YOUR CHILD CAN BE A G

Give your child the best pos
with an early learning scheme that's carefully planned,
tried and tested and, most of all, fun.

YOUR CHILD CAN BE A GENIUS, *and Happy!*

A practical guide for parents

Ken Adams

THORSONS PUBLISHING GROUP

First published 1988

© KEN ADAMS 1988

Illustrations by Marcus Byron

All rights reserved. No part of this book may be reproduced or utilized in any form or by any means electronic or mechanical, including photocopying, recording or by any information storage and retrieval system, without permission in writing from the Publisher.

British Library Cataloguing in Publication Data

Adams, Ken
Your child can be a genius – and happy! :
a practical guide for parents.
1. Exceptional children. Education
I. Title
371.9

ISBN 0-7225-1669-X

Published by Thorsons Publishers Limited,
Wellingborough, Northamptonshire, NN8 2RQ England.

Printed in Great Britain by Biddles Limited, Guildford, Surrey

3 5 7 9 10 8 6 4 2

CONTENTS

Introduction	7
Chapter	
1 Baby to Infant – 0-2 Years	17
2 The Adventurous Infant – 2-3 Years	49
3 The Agile Infant – 3-4 Years	75
4 Ready for School – 4-5 Years	103
5 Going to School – From 5 Years Onwards ...	131
In the Final Analysis	155
Index	157

INTRODUCTION

This book is in part inspired by my son, John, who recognized written words as a baby and learnt to read at two years of age. Up until then I had held firm to the idea that small children should be left to play; that they either could not or should not be taught anything before school age. I began to question this assumption because I now had a child of two who was obviously very ready to learn. In fact he seemed frustrated, climbing endlessly over the furniture in the front room and leaping off the dining-room table. He reminded me somewhat of a tiger at the Zoo, pacing to and fro in his cage over the same path, except that John was not caged physically. This was surely a symptom of mental frustration – he was begging for something to occupy his mind. Originally, I thought that reading would be the answer. If he could read those exciting stories about giants and witches for himself, then perhaps he would be satisfied.

I started teaching him to read, drawing on my own experiences as a teacher of non-English speaking Ugandan Asians in the 1970s, and he absorbed each short lesson at an amazing rate. By two-and-a-half years of age he was reading well enough to pick up almost any child's easy-to-read book and read it out loud with great expression.

In those pre-school years John's day was a long one. He woke at some unearthly hour of the morning and never went to sleep until very late in the evening, nearer midnight than eleven. However, the effect on his behaviour of the relatively short structured activity periods — about half an hour a day — was startling. It could have been coincidence, but from the start of the activity periods he became a calmer person. As he read for himself, John became more absorbed in the stories, drawn into a world of giants, goblins and witches. His eyes would light up with wonder as we turned the pages together and he could see and read about what the giant was doing, or whether poor Hansel was going to be eaten. He asked endless questions: 'How fast can the giant run? Will he catch Jack? His imagination was fired by those stories, he played games about them and read and re-read them again and again. He was a happy little two-year-old.

Later, when he was three, I decided to introduce more activities to stimulate and stretch his reasoning abilities. These activities were mainly in mathematics and English, plus some 'finding out' activities, and needed a considerable amount of organizing so that when he was finding one level of structured play easy there was another step that he could move onto that would stretch him further.

Apart from just reading, he wanted to count. He counted everything he saw – people in the street, cars, cows in the field in our village, even the tins of beans in the supermarket. At night I could hear him chattering away to himself, 'two hundred and four, two hundred and five . . .' He learned to tell the time, too, and within a couple of months he could work out the exact time, to the minute, from my watch.

When he was getting on for three years old I tried to get some 'expert' help for him. The children's doctor at the local clinic promised that she would find help, but came back to us a few weeks later despondent, and told us that there was none. The area psychologist seemed to think that this was all an exercise in 'come-uppance'; he could see no need for any special help. My wife and I were left to deal with a child with an excessively greedy mind: the more we fed it, the more it wanted. So we started to structure some of his daytime play, providing activities to stretch him intellectually. The activities had to be *play activities* which lasted only a short time and were fun. John seemed to need a succession of problems which he had a swift struggle to understand followed very quickly by finding a satisfactory solution. To him the activities were games, fascinating and absorbing. Before long he was reading almost everything he could lay his hands on, and through the structured steps of the mathematical games he developed mentally so fast that by the time the educational psychologist grudgingly decided that he could start school, John was already beyond primary-school level.

John went on to become, at nine-and-a-half years of age, the youngest child ever to pass Advanced Level GCE mathematics. He is quite capable of starting degree level mathematics, but he wishes to stay at his junior school. His two younger brothers also excel in school. Mark read at two and shows enormous potential at the age of six – he certainly could succeed like John before leaving primary school, and James, at eight, shows great promise in mathematics. All three are well ahead in their class and need to be set special work. Significantly though, all are also very sociable, exceptional at sports and rate 'mixing well' with other children as more important than succeeding academically. And they have friends of all types, bright and not-so-bright, sporty and not-so-sporty.

These, then, are children who have developed 'in the round'. Few restrictions have been placed on them either at home or at school (although a large family places its own restrictions on its members). Play was always an essential and pre-eminent part of their lives and still is. They are rumbustious, fun-loving, bossy with lively, enquiring minds. The only distinction between them and their schoolmates is that, in many respects, they are far ahead academically. They have confidence in themselves as far as schoolwork is concerned, and they are keen to pursue school-life to the full. They are happy 'geniuses', and around the country there must be hundreds, even thousands, who have great potential which has gone unrecognized both by their parents and even by their teachers. So many adults consider that the under-fives should not have their play structured in any way, but there is no reason why the intellectual needs of a generation of children should not be catered for through some structured, as well as unstructured, play. They will still be free to explore and have fun.

Why should I teach my child at home?

Some psychologists believe that the years between birth and starting school (0-5) are the most important years for the development of intelligence. If this is so then we, as parents should seek to provide an environment where:

- a child's language can develop through conversation, reading and writing;
- play activities can stimulate, challenge and develop a child's reasoning power (mathematical activities, for example, and encourage logical thinking;
- there are a wide variety of outlets for a child's needs to express himself in art, music and drama;
- activities are provided that will satisfy his 'scientific' need to investigate his world, to 'find out'.

However, we must remember that at this age children learn best through play and by using objects which are part of their everyday lives. They need 'concrete' experiences, interesting and challenging activities at which they can succeed and then go on eagerly to the next activity.

Numbers and counting for example can be learnt through handling real objects – toys, spoons, items of clothing. Your child's language will develop as you chat together during day-to-day activities, naming household objects, describing daily routines, singing bathtime songs, repeating goodnight rituals etc. He can 'find out' about volume or buoyancy as he plays in his bath, or 'helps' with the washing up. Even writing can be taught as a game so that his few minutes practice each day become something exciting he looks forward to.

The sort of structured play described in this book, even if it occupies no more than a few minutes per day, will help provide the foundations for patterns of thinking (for example, the development of logical thought through mathematical activities) and positive attitudes towards learning that will last a lifetime.

The time you spend together in conversation and the activities that you arrange for your child will strengthen the bond between you. You will gradually come to know and understand your child's individual intellectual needs; you will sense which activities will best extend him in a particular direction, or remedy a weakness, and still keep him happy and interested. At school, teacher-child contact time is limited because of class size; before school is the time to solve any fundamental problems through a one-to-one relationship which is relaxed and affectionate. Even an excellent teacher, with the best will in the world, cannot know a child in her class as you know your child, and certainly cannot always be on hand to answer questions, offer encouragement, or help with any difficulties.

In the home you can provide the many concrete learning experiences which will contribute in a very real way to the grasp of basic concepts and the depth of understanding that your child has of a subject like mathematics. These concrete learning experiences are time-consuming. In the years before school there is ample time to develop basic mathematical understanding, so that when your child does start school he can confidently approach new experiences in the classroom. You will also have the time in those early years to follow your child's progress closely and know how much practice and consolidation work he will need after learning a new skill or concept.

The parent is best placed to spot and nurture any special abilities a child may have. Some children show musical and artistic talents at a very young age, but mathematical and language gifts can go unnoticed, even by teachers. We have all read of great geniuses (Einstein, for example) who were not considered exceptional at school. This may be because they 'developed late', but it is more likely that their gifts were not recognized by their teachers. Most school systems for the primary child are designed for the average or rather bright child, and the activities and testing procedures will not discover the exceptional or 'gifted' child. Such children may be untidy in their work, disinterested in drawing pictures or producing well-presented topics or may even pay little attention to repetitive number work. Quite often parents who have helped their children over many years through play activities are in the best position to recognize that their child needs special help even though to teachers and educational psychologists this is not obvious.

The school, with its overstretched resources, cannot be expected to provide special facilities for gifted children. Such children need individual tuition, special books and equipment and at present the burden of supplying these falls mainly on the parent, and on a co-operative effort between parent and school. John, my son, has been lucky. His headteacher and a local authority advisor have arranged for special help in French and English, and he also has occasional use of a typewriter and special mathematics computer discs. But usually it is the parent who provides for music or art lessons for the artistically talented, or pays for extra tuition for a child who is talented in mathematics or English. There is often no real problem with children who are creatively precocious because such subjects do not cut across the school timetable to any great extent. But a child who is extremely advanced in mathematics, in particular, presents difficulties for primary school teachers who are often not able themselves to teach at this level.

Even an extremely bright child needs to take part in group activities, to be 'one of the crowd'. Too many solitary 'special' activities could make him feel isolated. However, if parents and school work together, if they regularly discuss the child's problems and progress, then he can be integrated into the school system; and if he has some special lessons throughout the week he will not be frustrated or underachieve.

Early learning through play activities may also be necessary for the happiness of the child. He may become bored and frustrated because he is not being stretched intellectually. Just extending the range of your child's experiences will add to his sense of fulfilment. A child, for example, who is ready to read at two years of age and yet is not taught to read until he is five, has missed three years of experiencing the joys of choosing and reading books for *himself*. Surely a child should learn when he is ready. If he is capable of solving mathematical problems and would derive great satisfaction from it, he should not be prevented from doing so just because he is only three years old.

The skills and the understanding that your child will gain through constructive play at home will also give him confidence when he does start school. He enjoys learning, he has made a good start in language and mathematics, and will therefore have confidence when he tackles these subjects at school. And if basic understanding and skills learned at school are supported by your interest and help at home, your child will be a happy and well-adjusted person in both environments.

The activities

The suggestions for activities are suggestions only. They are not a rigid timetable or a developmental checklist. They are ideas for ways of helping your child develop his potential at his own pace, be he a highflyer, average, or finding difficulty with certain aspects of, say, learning to sort by colour.

Do remember that most children will only get as far as counting, recognizing numbers and some letters, and writing their names by the time they start school at four to five years of age.

Some children are capable of achieving far more than this before they start school. If so, the activities suggested in this book will help them.

The important thing to remember is to take your cue and pace from your child. Never force any activity on him or make him wrestle with one which is too difficult. You will know him well enough to recognize signs of boredom, frustration or resentment. Little and often is the maxim, followed closely by making sure that he has understood each step before he moves on to the next.

The activities have been graded according to age. This age is a rough guide only; your child will make it obvious when he needs a more demanding activity or when he is struggling.

The activities do follow a logical developmental sequence, especially those aimed at developing early mathematical concepts, so even if your child is working on activities designed for an older or younger child, do make sure you follow the sequence within that age group. For example, your child will need to be able to sound fluently and recognize number symbols before you try to introduce simple addition sums.

At all times take your cue and pace from him. Young

children learn through enjoyment and success. Repeated failure or pressure to begin or continue an activity which he finds difficult or boring will only undermine enjoyment and confidence and might eventually lead him to reject any activity you offer.

For example, you might decide to see if he wants to build a tower with playcups. To begin with he may just want to explore the cups. The box they came in may well provide many happy minutes or hours of play as he learns to open and close it, to take the cups out and try to stuff them back in again. He may want to play with them as cups, put things in them, throw them, have them in the bath and generally find out all the various interesting possibilities they offer. This stage might last a few minutes or a few days. This kind of unstructured, exploratory play is vital for a young child and should take precedence over structured activities.

When he shows an interest in piling them up, you should show him how to build a tower, talking to him all the time about how you are putting the biggest cup on the bottom and gradually building upwards to the smallest one on the top. Perhaps you could make up a song about what you are doing, using the words 'big' or 'biggest' and 'small' or 'smallest'. When you have finished the tower, take it down and ask him to help you build the next one. You can sort through the cups together, asking him to find out the biggest cup, and gradually working up to the smallest. Then take the tower down and ask him to do it on his own. If you start with just three cups he will find it easier to grasp both the basic physical principles and perhaps even the language to express those principles. For example, he might call the cups the 'daddy' (biggest) cup, the 'mummy' (middle-size) cup, and the 'baby' (smallest) cup. Stories like 'Goldilocks and the Three Bears' or 'The Three Billy Goats Gruff' will reinforce both the language and the ideas of comparative size.

This example shows that for your child to build a tower he needs to be able to:

- grasp the basic principle that the biggest cup goes on the bottom and the smallest on top;

- use the physical (or 'motor') skills to pick up the cups

and place them on top of each other without knocking them over;

- if possible, use language to explain what he is doing and name the concepts he is learning: biggest, middle-size, smallest; on top, on the bottom etc.

Obviously the third point, the language, will be the last to come and may well be in the crude form of: 'Daddy cup, Mummy cup, baby cup' but it shows that he has understood and really grasped what building a tower is all about.

This example shows how the activities can be used. The suggestions given in the following chapters are, as it were, the bare bones, which need to be fleshed out by you, as you know your child best. The important thing is to introduce activities at the appropriate time, when your child will be ready for them. In the example above, for instance, there would be little point in introducing the tower-building activity until your child had finished exploring the cups and was able to pick them up and distinguish between the different sizes.

The other important aspect is language. Even when your child is very young, talk to him during each activity, explain what you are doing, what you want him to do. Introduce songs, stories, rhymes which are appropriate. Although when he is very young he will copy your actions rather than follow verbal instructions, he will be absorbing vocabulary and learning that language is a way of explaining and making sense of the world.

The sequence of activities

In each chapter the activities are given in the same broad sequence: talking or language; mathematics; reading; exploring/finding out activities, creative play; other activities. Remember: language will underpin all the other activities so do talk to your child during the activities and give him a chance to respond and ask questions.

Timing

You should introduce the activities when your child seems ready for them. The ages given are a guide: your child may well be working on one level for reading and another for mathematics.

He may need minutes, days, weeks to grasp a certain point. Do make sure that he really understands one activity before you go on to the next. Just because he managed to complete an activity successfully does not necessarily mean he has understood it, or that he will remember it the next day. From time to time, go back to an earlier activity, partly to revise it but also to boost his confidence.

Enjoyment

Above all, your child should enjoy the activities. At this age your child is developing many different skills. He will enjoy this development if he is allowed to develop at his own pace and to his own level. The activities in this book will help you to help him to do this.

CHAPTER 1
BABY TO INFANT –
0-2 YEARS

I remember the day, when my son John was ten months old, a neighbour's child came skipping into the kitchen and proclaimed excitedly, 'He can say the words without the pictures!'. All the family rushed into the living room to test the truth of such a remarkable statement, myself included (I remember thinking 'this is nonsense'). But there was no doubting the fact: our young baby could most certainly recognize several words with pictures. At that moment my whole pattern of thinking about babies and infants was turned on its head. Previously, I considered that babies and pre-school children should be allowed to develop physically and have *fun*. But, just suppose that the next four or five years were going to be a time of intellectual frustration for John, as well as a time of play, exploration and fun? I reasoned that, if nothing else, he should be provided with the sort of environment that would allow him to develop to his full potential intellectually as well as physically and socially; and he would still have *fun*.

This all led to the development of structured play for each of our children as they came to this age. It allowed for a considerable amount of exploring play and free choice, but within the 'play' time certain activities were introduced according to what we considered were our child's intellectual needs. At all times play was considered to be one of the most effective kinds of learning. The emphasis was on enjoyment, and the activities lasted only as long as the baby's concentration span, interest and enjoyment. At this stage of a child's development there are several key factors to be borne in mind when deciding how best to help your child:

- A young child learns best from practical, 'concrete' experiences: for example, he will learn to count best by counting real things around the house, at the supermarket and along the street. He needs to *feel* the roundness of a ball, rather than just look at a one-dimensional picture in a book.
- His speech and vocabulary are beginning to develop. They will develop best where adults (and older children in the family) communicate well but naturally with the child.
- He is finding different ways of exploring. You will have to provide the materials for learning.
- Once he has learnt a skill, or grasped an idea through an experience, he will need to use that knowledge to reach towards higher levels of understanding. Through your special relationship with your child you can provide new and challenging experiences for him.
- Every child is an individual: what suits one child may not suit another, even at the same stage of development. For example, different children often learn the same skill or concept from totally different toys, and have very definite preferences for those toys.

The early years are important years for building the foundations of human intelligence, and you will have to decide what activities are appropriate to your child's needs and how those activities can best be fitted into his daily routine. Some of the activities may well be beyond his range, others will not; and for a very few children (the so-called 'gifted') certain groups of activities will not go far enough, at least in this chapter. By patient investigation you can decide, for example, whether a jigsaw of a few pieces is within the capability of your child. In trying him with various activities there must be no suggestion of force or pressure, however, your child will indicate quite clearly if he is 'ready' for the activity or not. At all times take the cue and the pace from him. For example, you might decide to see if he can build a tower with playcups. You show him first what to do. You put the largest on the bottom and build upwards to the smallest at the top. Then you take down the tower and put the cups in a pile and ask him to build the same tower. If he can't distinguish between biggest and smallest he will pick any cup at random and start with that, sometimes trying to place a bigger cup on top of a smaller. If after two or three tries of patient demonstration he still cannot build the tower you should assume that he is not 'ready' for that activity, leave it and come back and try again in a few weeks time. Similarly, an eighteen-month-old child is sometimes 'ready' to build a simple bridge with three bricks after being shown, but it is rare to find a twelve-month-old child who can do this even after being shown how several times.

Finally, I must emphasize that whatever activities you decide to introduce, do allot a very large proportion of the time to 'exploring' play so that any playtime should include the mastering of 'motor' skills, recalling events by using objects to represent real things (for example, using marbles as men to drive toy lorries), and social games. All forms of play should be allowed to develop freely and spontaneously alongside the parent-organized activities because they will be essential to the full and 'rounded' development of your child.

ACTIVITIES FOR 0-2 YEARS

Most of the activities suggested in this chapter will be appropriate for a child of between one and two years of age, especially a child of nearly two (rising-two). Many a rising-two is hyperactive and his desire to explore often drives his parents to distraction so this is the age for which this chapter will be particularly appropriate. I include a short table of developmental stages so that you can gauge when your child might be able to perform certain activities. For example, he will have difficulty with the 'stepping' activity if he has only just learned to walk. Also bear in mind that young children vary greatly in their rate of physical development (for example children can begin walking as early as eight months or as late as eighteen months); and there is an even greater variation in their mental development.

Development 0-2 years

- Five months: can sit straight if pulled into a sitting position.
- Six months: can grasp a cube block.
- One year: can stand and walk a few steps. First words spoken. Similar sound and vision to an adult.
- One to two years: trial and error learning. Making words and gestures. Knows own name. Difficulty with some vowel sounds.
- Eighteen months on: can walk up stairs and run and pick up things easily.
- Two years on: Is now definitely right- or left-handed. Builds a tower quite easily. Speaks short sentences. Dresses up. Still not social in play with other children.

Talking

This is the time when your baby will start talking. At one year of age he may say one or two words, or make rather odd sounds like 'leedle, leedle, leedle'; he is testing out his tongue and experimenting. You perhaps have noticed that your child repeats a particular sound that he likes over and over again. In the first place he makes these sounds because he hears someone speaking, so he tries to do the same thing. He is learning by imitation and repetition and he learns best when you communicate with him.

Conversation is tremendously important but it must be natural. Talk to him as you go about your daily routine. Talk to him as you walk about the house doing things – tell him what you are doing and why. Talk to him as you carry him around with you, as you do the shopping, as you bath him, as you carry him upstairs to tuck him up in bed. Ask him questions: 'Are you hungry?'; 'Would you like a biscuit?'; 'What do you want to do now?'; 'Do you want chips for dinner?'; 'Where are your shoes?'

Explain things

Tell him why you are doing things: 'We are going to the shops to get some food to make dinner'; 'We have to put away your toys or someone may trip over them'; 'We have to wash your hands because they're dirty'. Try to accompany explanations with gestures and actions which make the words more meaningful.

Point out things

At this stage he needs all the naming words he can absorb. Start with things he sees or uses every day:

- *Things on the face*: eyes, mouth, ears, nose, teeth, chin, hair.
- *Parts of the body*: arms, legs, hands, feet, fingers, toes, tummy, chest, bottom, head.
- *Clothes*: vest, pants, socks, tights, shirt, blouse, skirt, dress, trousers, coat, sweater, hat, scarf, gloves, shoes, boots, etc.
- *Food*: potatoes, meat, cheese, milk, cornflakes, sugar, egg, cake, biscuits, orange, apple, nuts, bananas, etc.
- *Things around the house*: door, window, table, chair, book, television (TV), fridge, plate, knife, fork, spoon, cup, toilet, potty, etc.
- *Things in the street*: lorry, car, house, bicycle, man, woman, bus, postman, wall, tree, grass, dog, cat, etc.
- *On the TV*: news, funny man, singer, dancer, football, cricket, ball, cartoon, etc.

The list is almost endless. There is so much to talk about, so much to learn. But don't assume that your child is bored simply because you have told him about the same thing for several days running; children need and love repetition. They need to practise each new skill, including listening and especially talking.

Play with bricks and the posting-box

At this young age children learn about the physical world by actually exploring it through play. By handling bricks of different sizes and shapes they are not only improving their physical co-ordination as they learn to place bricks on top of each other, or arrange them in a line, but they are also finding out about size, shape and weight. As they try to build towers, or to fit bricks in a posting box they are absorbing certain basic physical rules about the world in which they live. And if they have absorbed these rules through concrete experience at this age, they will find it far easier to grasp the corresponding abstract principles as they grow older. For example, handling a spherical brick or a round ball, rolling it along the floor, trying to build with it or post it through a hole will teach a child all about the properties of spheres which he will then go on to explore in a different way in geometry or art at a later age.

Concept of size

What you need

- A set of cuboid-shaped bricks of different sizes: wooden ones are better to build with. Choose plain wood or coloured ones.
- A set of bricks of various shapes: cuboids, cylinders, prisms, various other solid shapes.
- Plastic cups that fit inside each other: cylindrical ones are easier to use.

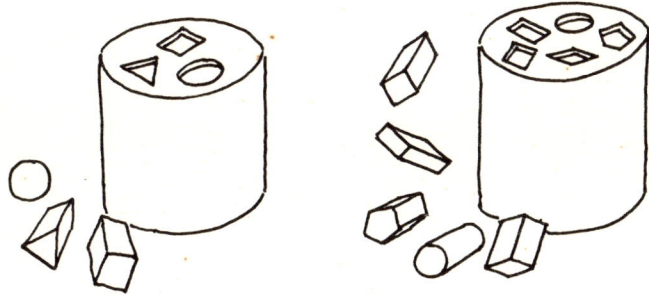

- Different posting boxes of varying degrees of difficulty: the type needed will depend on your child's age and stage of development.

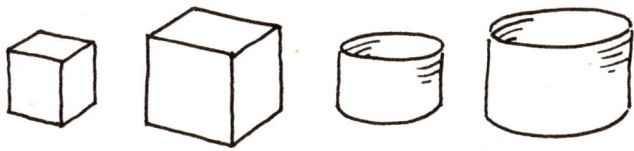

What to do

- Take two cuboid bricks - one large, one small. Talk about the different sizes: 'This is the big brick. Look, you can only just hold it in your hand. This is the little brick - you can hold it easily. I'm going to put them here. This is the big brick (pointing) and this is the little brick (pointing). Let's mix them up. Now, can you put the big brick here? And can you put the little brick here?' If he cannot do it after a couple of tries, abandon the project and leave it until another day. If he finds it easy, then increase the number of bricks until he can *just* do it.

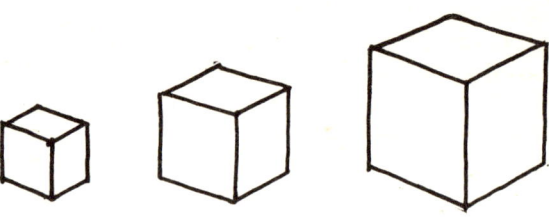

- Ask your child to make a 'train'. The largest brick will be the engine and the other bricks will be the carriages, ranging down in size to the guard's van at the end.

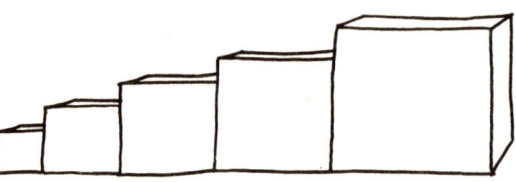

If you think your child will understand, you can introduce words such as big, bigger, biggest and small, smaller, smallest. Your set of bricks may include long, thin bricks, so that you can vary the game with long, longer, longest and short, shorter, shortest. However, the idea is to introduce the concept of *ordering by size*, so don't labour over words. He will find the word side of the exercise easier in a year or two.

- *Building towers* Your child can use bricks or cups of various sizes. Explain what you want him to do (see p.14), and then show him how to build a tower with the biggest brick at the bottom and the smallest on top. Start with three bricks or cups and, according to your child's ability, increase the number.

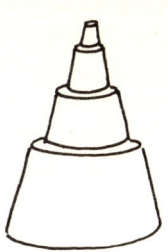

- *Fitting cups inside each other* Reverse the cups and fit them one inside another. Show your child how to do this at first, and then let him do it. Start with just two cups, then gradually build up the number. As previously, explain what you are doing: 'Look, I can put this little cup inside this one. And I can put this cup inside this one. Can you do it?'

- *Which is the middle one?* Arrange three equal-sized bricks in a line. Say: 'This is the middle one', and point. Move the bricks around and put them in a line again. Point out the middle brick again. Do this several times and then ask him: 'Which is the middle one?'. Don't worry if he doesn't understand at first, but come back to the game a few days later. You can also introduce the idea of two 'ends' with three bricks. Games which emphasize 'middle' which he may enjoy playing are 'Piggy in the middle' (use a balloon or soft sponge ball) or making sandwiches —either food or human!

- *Building a bridge* Obviously before your child can build a bridge he will have to know what a bridge is, so make sure he has had plenty of time to play at pushing his cars or other toys under bridges, or crawled through a bridge you make by standing with your legs apart, or by joining hands with another adult. 'The Three Billy Goats Gruff' and songs like 'London Bridge is falling down' can help here. When you think he is ready for the actual physical activity of building a bridge, put some cuboid-shaped bricks on the floor. Ask your child to build a bridge. A rising-two can usually manage to do this, but a younger child may need to be shown how first. Allow some time for thought because very bright children may want to build an elaborate bridge.

Sorting

Sorting or grouping similar objects is useful concrete experience for learning to group similar numbers, as for example in learning times tables, or addition. Once your child has grasped the idea of sorting very different objects, eg: sorting socks and jumpers for washing, or sorting tins and fresh vegetables after shopping, or biscuits and sandwiches at tea, then he can be taught how to sort similar objects on the basis of first shape, and then perhaps colour.

By shape

Put two cuboid bricks and two cylindrical bricks in a pile. Try to make sure they are all the same colour and about the same size. Say: 'We're going to put the bricks into families. All these bricks (point to the cuboid bricks) live here; and all these bricks (point to the cylindrical bricks) live here.' Then mix the bricks up and ask him to do it. If he cannot, then show him at first. If he can do it easily, then introduce larger quantities of bricks and then gradually introduce more shapes, but only bring in one new shape at a time.

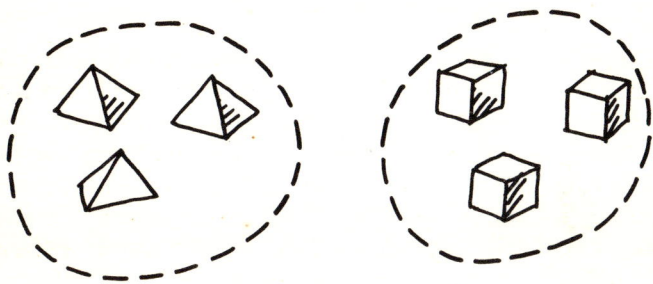

By colour
Repeat the sorting process, but show your child how to sort on the basis of colour. Obviously, you will need several bricks of at least two different colours, and until your child recognizes colours this exercise will be meaningless.

If at any point he sorts correctly, but not on the basis that you have explained, do not check him but say, 'Good. Now see if you can do it this way.'

Again, don't labour over the game or exercise when it is obvious that your child is finding it too difficult. Leave it, go on to something else, and come back a few days later.

By pattern
Lay out the bricks in an a/b, a/b pattern as shown below. As you do so, explain to your child what you are doing: 'First I put down one of these bricks, then one of these, then one of these. What one do I put down next?' If your child can work out which kind of brick comes next quite easily before the age of two, he is probably ready for the problem-solving games on p.45-48.

Reading to your child

The foundations for learning to read are laid in the home almost as soon as your baby is born. If your house is a place where songs, rhymes, jingles, stories and books of all sorts are an essential part of everyday life then your child's enjoyment of all these from the earliest age is the best motivation for mastering print.

You should aim to have children's books of all sorts in the house – old ones, new ones, picture books, nursery rhyme books, fiction and non-fiction. And you don't have to spend a fortune buying them. We went 'book hunting' for our small children year after year to jumble sales and fêtes. Eventually, there were good books everywhere – on the bookcase, on shelves, on tables in most rooms, in the toy box, in boxes under the bed and in cardboard boxes in cupboards and on the bedroom floor. At bedtime there were books of every type readily available. In the daytime, we made sure that there were books to hand so that the children could always browse whenever they wanted.

Most libraries now have special sections for under-fives and children can join at very young ages (provided, of course, that you make sure the books are returned in good condition.)

Choosing books

When choosing a book for your child do remember that reading it has to be a *shared* experience. You read to him, but he will want to comment on what you are reading. He may be interested in *how* you say something: perhaps he will copy you. For example, I found that all my children loved to repeat 'Fee, Fi, Fo, Fum...' from *Jack and the Beanstalk*, and 'You can't catch me, I'm the Gingerbread Man' – an equally popular story. And very young children love to try out finger rhymes like 'Round and round the garden, like a teddy bear' on *you* and see how *you* react.

Pictures are an important part of the story at this age. They give clues as to what is happening and offer endless food for questions and discussion. Once they have heard a story, children often spend hours poring over the illustrations, re-creating the story in their heads or, with younger children, out loud.

In the beginning you might point things out in the pictures and ask questions: 'Look! isn't the giant big? He's much bigger than the man, isn't he? Is the giant as big as a tree do you think?' You can illustrate your words with actions: 'Jack is as big as *this*, and the giant is as big as *this*' (using your hands to show how far off the ground they are.) By doing this, not only will you bring the story to life but you are also offering vocabulary which your child can use both to answer your questions and to ask ones of his own.

Make sure when you choose a book that you choose it for *your* child. Ask yourself: 'Will he be interested? The language is simple enough but does it follow? The pictures are marvellous but is the story any good?' Imagine that you are reading it to him. Try and decide how your shared reading and experience will develop as you read the story. Only then should you decide whether or not to take the plunge and buy it.

Where and when to read

Finally, when you read to your child, do make sure that you both enjoy it as much as possible by choosing somewhere comfortable. Most children will want to sit on your lap or at least have your arm around them so that you can enjoy close physical contact and see the words and pictures clearly. Do, from time to time, run your fingers under the words as you read. This will help convey the idea that the message is in the print and that the message has to be read from left to right and from the top to bottom of the page. (Don't try to sound out the words one at a time as your finger lands on them or fluency and expression will be lost.)

Read to your child every day, and with as much expression as you can, so that he gets a sense of the excitement, the wonder of stories. A giant, for example, demands a giant-like voice, slow and tremendous (please don't scare the neighbours though!). To a small child the expression in your voice means more than the words: watch how his eyes light up as your voice rises and falls with the mood of the story!

Story books can be about real life or giants, witches and goblins. Small children seem to act out both types of stories in their games. If you are ever at a loss for a 'good read' ask at your local library. Not only will they have a suggested reading list for under-fives but will also be able to recommend books similar to ones that you and your child may have read and enjoyed together.

Rhymes

Even the youngest children seem to love rhymes. You will probably remember several from your own childhood. If you can't, or if you would like to extend your repertoire, you should be able to find good collections of these rhymes in your local library.

Finger rhymes
'Round and round the garden (*run your finger round and round your child's palm*)
Like a teddy bear
One step, two step (*walk your fingers up his arm*)
Tickly under there (*tickle under arm*).

This little piggy went to market (*hold his little finger*)
This little piggy stayed at home (*waggle the next finger*)
This little piggy had roast beef (*the next finger*)
This little piggy had none (*the next finger*)
This little piggy went 'whee, whee'
All the way home (*waggle the thumb, and run up the arm to tickle*).

Counting and acting rhymes

1, 2, 3, 4, 5,
Once I caught a fish alive
6, 7, 8, 9, 10
Then I let it go again.

I'm a little teapot
Short and stout (*stoop down*)
Here's my handle (*bend arm in to make a handle*)
Here's my spout (*put other arm out to make a spout*)
When it comes to tea-time
Hear me shout
Tip me up (*tip up with one foot off the floor*)
And pour me out.

Incy Wincy Spider
Climbing up the spout (*wiggle your fingers as you move them up*)
Down came the rain (*wiggle your fingers downward*)
And washed the spider out
Out came the sun (*spread your arms outward*)
And dried up all the rain
Incy Wincy Spider
Climbing up again (*wiggle your fingers as you move your hands up*).

Jelly on a plate
Jelly on a plate
Wibble-wobble (*wiggle about like wobbly jelly*)
Wibble-wobble
Jelly on a plate.

Lick two pieces of paper (or make finger puppets) and put them on your index fingers for:

Two little dicky birds
Sitting on a wall
One named Peter
One named Paul
Fly away Peter (*put index finger behind head and re-show middle finger*)
Fly away Paul (*same with other index finger*)
Come back Peter
Come back Paul (*bring back both index fingers to show the stuck-on bits of paper*).

Babies of about a year old are particularly keen on:

Pat-a-cake,
Pat-a-cake, Baker's man (*pat the palms of your hands with your baby's*)
Bake me a cake as fast as you can
Pat it and prick it and mark it with B
And put it in the oven for you and for me (*point to him and then to yourself*).

Our children gurgled with delight at this one from six months to two years old.

Nursery rhymes

Besides acting and singing rhymes there are the standard nursery rhymes which small children have never tired of over the centuries. They are a must for frequent reading and chanting and you will be amazed at how young an age a child can recite several full-length nursery rhymes. Some children can recite 'Jack and Jill' before they can ask for their shoes to be done up. One of the reasons that children are so fascinated by nursery rhymes is because they love repetition. Be warned: you may read a favourite rhyme or story a thousand times and your child will still want to hear it again!

Records, tapes and television programmes

Your local children's library should have a good stock of records and tapes of nursery rhymes and jingles which you can play for your child when your vocal chords and patience are exhausted! These rhymes and jingles have all the ingredients — rhyme, rhythm and repetition — which make them so enjoyable for young children and so easy to learn. Through listening, learning and repeating them your child is practising all the skills he needs to master both English and perhaps later a foreign language. A 'good' ear for languages is often the result of years of having learned how to listen carefully.

There are also a good many pre-school television programmes that might suit your child. Make a list of all the relevant programmes and make a point of watching them together. Talk to him both before the programme about what it might be about, and afterwards about what it actually was about, whether he enjoyed it, which bits he liked most, etc. Encourage him to think and talk about the programmes so that watching television becomes an active, interesting experience rather than a passive one. Observe his reactions during the programme and cross off the list any which he finds boring.

Pre-reading activities

At this age, the most important preparation for learning to read is for your child to be surrounded by books, read to whenever possible, and for him to enjoy stories rhymes and jingles.

Some children show signs of wanting to learn what the letters and words say: they may point to words as you read or pick out print on cereal packets, the on/off switch on the washing machine, push/pull signs on doors etc. If your child does this, he may enjoy activities with flash cards.

Reading cards

What you need
Cut out pieces of white card. Either paste on cut-out pictures of common, everyday objects or draw and colour pictures straight onto the card. Write the word for the picture in large, clear letters above or beneath the picture. *Don't* use capitals at this stage. Use 'script' or print letters as shown below:

a b c d e f g h i j k l m n o p q r s t u v w x y z

What you do
Show your child the reading cards daily, saying the word out loud as he looks at the picture. Point at the word and say it again. Try to encourage him to repeat it, but don't press the issue. Soon he will be saying the word as soon as he picks up the card. Make a game of it by letting him keep the card when he says the word. Start with just one or two cards, and make sure the words look and sound very different, e.g. cat, dog, pin, so that they are very distinct.

Eventually, you might try covering up the picture and just showing the word. If your child does not recognize the word, don't worry. Just go back to showing picture and word together, and come back to covering up the picture a few weeks later. Just bear in mind that when he can recognize the word without the picture he is near the stage of 'readiness to read' and for some children this may be from age three years on. In any event, as the weeks go by extend the variety of the cards, but only include nouns.

Exploring play

Young children learn about the world they live in by exploring it through play. At this young age their play is very physical. They are learning to control their body movements as they try to pour liquids, roll a ball of Plasticine, fill a cup with sand or put a small toy inside a saucepan and then take it out again. But these early explorations with sand, water, volume, buoyancy, etc. are also the beginnings of scientific experiment, the desire to find out 'what will happen if?' They are learning to experiment, observe and formulate rules based on their observations. All this may seem a far cry from the mess in your kitchen and bathroom but only through such mess will your young child have the chance to enjoy the concrete experiences which underpin much mathematical and scientific thinking.

Water

What you need
A bowl half-full of water, some things (e.g., toys) that float, some that sink, plastic cups of different sizes. In summer the bowl can be outside on a concrete path or patio. In bad weather your child can stand on a chair up at the kitchen sink.

What to do
Show him that some things stay on top of the water and others sink. Leave him to investigate and play (rising-twos). Show him how to use a small plastic cup to fill up a large one. What happens when he fills a large cup and tries to pour the water from it into a small one?

Let him play freely with toys and floating objects in his bath and in the bowl. A lot of splashing may ensue!

Sand

The beach is the best place for a child to experiment with sand, using a bucket and spade for example. At home you can make or buy a sand tray.

What you need
Buy a flat sand tray (a large cat-litter tray would do) and a small pack of sand (about three kilos should be enough to start with). Spread out some newspaper on a concrete patio (or a large polythene sheet indoors) and put the sand tray on top of it. If he plays with the sand outside, do check carefully to make sure animals don't soil it.

What you do
As with water, your child can investigate various sizes of containers (use plastic cups, not glass!) to discover how much sand can be transferred from one to another. Help him a little, then leave him to experiment and find out about quantity for himself.

Plasticine, Play-Doh

Use a wooden board or plastic tray on a table. Put the Plasticine or Play-Doh on the board, and show your child how to make a sphere by rolling it in his hands; how to make a cylindrical shape by pressing and rolling on the board. Provide him with a *blunt* knife to cut the Plasticine.

Now leave him to experiement. If he wants suggestions, show him how to make a snake, a snowman, 'food' –

sausages, peas, cakes, etc. If he is very dextrous and ambitious, show him how to make a little house and garden of trees and flowers with different coloured Plasticine.

Pots, pans and wooden spoons

Your child can have huge amounts of fun with pots, pans, saucepan lids, colanders and wooden spoons, and small toys that he can put into and take out of the containers.

Marbles, toy cars

Play the 'which will go the furthest?' game. Roll the marbles or push the car along the floor.

How far has each one gone?

Measure the distance by 'stepping and counting'.

Creative play

'Creative play' covers a wide range of activities through which your child can explore himself by exploring his feelings and acting out his fantasies. It will include drawing, painting, dressing-up and acting, dancing, making music and, later on, writing.

A young child's creativity can be stifled if he is not left to his own devices. He may well need help with some of the physical skills but you should not attempt to direct what he does with those skills unless he asks for advice. So, for example, by all means show him how to hold a crayon to make a scribble (rising-two), but do not try to show him how to draw anything in particular.

Drawing and painting

What you need
Large crayons (short, wax ones are best), sugar paper; some rising-twos may be able to cope with paints (small quantities of powder paint are best) and some may enjoy packets of stick-paper shapes.

What to do
Let him kneel up at a well-protected table covered either in double-newspaper or polythene. Give him one activity at a time.

- *Drawing* Show him how to hold the crayon and how to make marks on the paper. Then leave him to experiment.
- *Painting* Find an old overall or shirt he can put on before letting him paint: make it part of an exciting game – 'dressing-up' for painting. Mix small quantities of paint on plates (so the paint can't get spilt.)

You will have to be with him at the beginning to show him what to do. Brushes may be a little difficult so show him how to dip a finger into one colour paint and make a mark on the sugar paper. Invite him to do the same. When he has got the idea, and knows that he can paint lines, do squiggles, curves and dots, leave him to do his own picure. From the beginning make sure that he tells you when he has finished, otherwise he will get down from the table with wet, painted fingers and cheerfully mark your door, the wall and anything else within reach!

Sticky-shape pictures

A two-year-old can be shown how to stick shapes onto paper and then be left to experiment. This can be one of the really quiet and peaceful activities, but watch out for sticky shapes on the furniture, on his face, on the cat if he is left for too long. (As ever, be suspicious of peace and quiet for too long!)

For a rising-two a pack which includes small shapes (triangles, squares, rectangles and circles) is useful, and gives a very early introduction to geometry. The idea is to give him freedom in what he does on the sugar paper, but it is helpful if you show him at first how to put the individual shapes on. As you stick a circle on the paper say: 'This is a circle'. Do the same with the other shapes, but don't labour over naming too much. This is intended to be very much a play activity at this stage and later on (Chapters 2 and 3) you can introduce patterns, symmetry and numbers of sides. Another tip: buy a few sheets of large-squared graph paper and let him stick the shapes on this as well.

Dressing-up and acting

At some time towards the end of this age range the acting

flair will begin to show – in some children more than others. Some small children will take part in copying what adults do (with or without other children), pretending to be daddy doing the gardening or mummy driving the car. He may put on daddy's Wellington boots to pretend to be a giant. Now is the time to start collecting old clothes from fêtes and jumble sales. Start a 'dressing-up' box now, and by school age it will be pretty full.

Dressing-up clothes

Straw hats, a trilby, old cloaks (or long pieces of material for use as cloaks), caps, jackets of all sizes, long dresses, extravagant hats, bags, jewellery; anything that can be used to dress up as a pirate, a Red Indian, a cowboy or any other hero or superhero you can think of. The best thing is to watch the television and see what cartoon series is currently the craze.

Dancing

One of the activities best loved by children at this age is listening and dancing to jingles and children's songs on record and tape. My children had no hesitation in jigging to all sorts of bouncy tunes, and one took great delight in getting up on the dining-room table to do his dance!

Most of our children's records came from jumble sales, but you really need just one good record or tape of children's songs and rhymes to keep him happy for a very long time.

Many libraries now stock children's tapes and records. As with favourite rhymes, you will probably be driven frantic by *The runaway train* or *Old MacDonald had a farm*, with all the accompanying noises, day after day, but your child will love them; he will never tire of the constant repetition.

If your child likes a different approach, line up some teddy bears or dolls and he can 'dance' them to the tunes. This will help him sort out the different 'moods' of music (sad, happy) and also the varying rhythms. You can help by tapping out the rhythm with a ruler on the top of a table.

Music

What you need
Pots, pans, wooden spoons, toy xylophone, plastic trumpet, etc.

What you do
Simply allow your child to experiment, as long as he doesn't hurt himself. And make sure that your neighbour is not on night-shift before the funs begins.

Counting

Start by counting the stairs as you take your child up to bed. It is best, at first, to count only five steps, perhaps the last five at the top. Count loudly 'one, two, three, four, five'. Try to get him to count with you, but don't worry if he doesn't respond at first.

On fingers

Some rhymes are useful, e.g., *This little piggy went to market* and *One, two, three, four, five*. Count on your baby's fingers or toes as you recite or sing the rhyme.

At home

Count the windows, chairs in the room, doors, legs on a chair, toys.
- *At the table* count cakes or biscuits on a plate, cutlery, tableware.

- *At the supermarket* Let your child count how many things you have in your basket.
- *Counting with buttons* If your child sits at the table you can lay out buttons in front of him and count out together.

The emphasis at this stage must be on just counting: do not introduce the written numbers. Counting, like reading, must be an enjoyable part of everyday life.
- *Counting bricks* Let him build a tower of bricks and try to count how many. He can also try making a long line of bricks on the floor and counting those. Count with him as much as you can. When he can count no further, carry on and tell him the next couple of numbers.

- *Counting steps* Ask your child: 'How far can you get if you take three very big steps?' Count with him as he steps out. Now you step out three steps, counting aloud.

Repeat with five steps. Also ask him to count how many big steps it takes to get across a room or from one door to another: count out loudly and clearly with him.

How far you take the counting depends on your child. Make every activity enjoyable, a game which lasts as long as his interest allows. Remember the maxim: little and often if best (*often* meaning at least once a day).

Labelling and colour cards

Labelling cards

It will help to develop your child's vocabulary and reading readiness if you start now by labelling some of the objects around the house. Begin with just a few objects: door, bed, chair, window. After a couple of weeks add more labels: plate, spoon, cup, potty. Put the labels at his eye-level. From time to time, and in a natural way as you both meet up at a label, just point to it and say: 'That says door. This is a door.' Eventually, you will have many labels around the house and your child will know the names of the objects though not at first the words.

Name tags are even more important; they contribute to your child's feeling of his own importance. So put a few labels on some of his things: toys, clothes, books. For example, write 'James' with the capital letter first and lower-case letters after, as you would usually write his name.

Occasionally pick up a toy or book and say, 'This says James. This is James's toy.'

Colour Cards

What you need
Some old playing cards, coloured sticky paper — blue, green, red, yellow, orange, purple or (violet).

What you do
Cut the coloured paper to fit over the cards: make several of each colour. For the very young child (about eighteen months upwards), you can begin 'teaching' colours. The main colours to learn are red, orange, yellow, green, blue and purple (or violet).

For several weeks before starting this activity, make a point of emphasizing colour as you talk together: 'You've got your red socks on today'; 'Where's your blue car?'; 'Look at that black dog', etc. Sing songs about colours and pick out books which emphasize colour either in the story or the illustration.

Colours are best taught one at a time. If you decide to start with RED then take your red card and say: 'This is the colour red'. Ask him: 'Is there anything else red in the room?' If he doesn't understand what you mean, then point out some objects which are red. The difficulty at this stage is to communicate the idea of redness, which is tricky, especially where there are so many *shades* of red. Try him with the same 'game' for a few minutes, or longer if he is very keen. If he does manage to pick out something red then praise him: 'Well done, that is very good. You clever boy.' In any case, leave the activity after a few minutes, and return to it the next day. However he gets on say, 'Well done, you have done very well. Good boy.' Don't be disappointed if he doesn't get the idea of redness, even for some weeks. You must be patient. The activity must be kept at his own relaxed pace, with no suggestion of pressure.

Meanwhile, make a point of mentioning red when it crops up naturally: 'Do you want your red ball?', 'Would you like the red mug?', 'Where are your red gloves?'. Introduce only one colour at a time.

Once he knows two or more colours, for a game mix up all the cards into the colour groups he knows. Then see if he can name the colours in each group. Help him if he can't do it fairly quickly.

Problem-solving

Many young children develop a keen sense of humour very early on in life. They enjoy absurd situations and love to be able to point out when something has gone wrong and how to put it right. Their enjoyment shows that they have grasped the basic principles involved in putting on certain clothes, eating certain foods with certain implements etc. At this young age the 'problems' need to be everyday ones which include familiar objects.

Things to do

A good way to begin might be to put clothes on back to front or on the wrong part of the body. This is a game you can play together as you get dressed in the morning or before you go out. For example:

• When getting him dressed in the morning, try putting his socks on his hands or pants on his head and ask: 'Is this right? Does this go here?'
• When you are getting ready to go out, try putting his hat on his hands or his socks on his ears! Ask again: 'Is this right? Does this go here?'
• Move on to household objects; trying brushing his hair with his toothbrush or cleaning his teeth with his flannel. Ask again: 'Am I using the right brush?'
If he enjoys this game, move on gradually to other

'deliberate' mistakes, but this time see if he can *explain* why something is wrong:
- Try putting a jumper on upside down. Ask: 'Why can't I put my jumper on?'
- Try brushing his hair with the wrong end of the brush. Ask him: 'Why is your hair still messy?'
- Try to pour milk out of an unopened bottle or carton. Ask him: 'Why won't the milk come out?'
- Try to eat yogurt with a fork. Ask him: 'Why can't I eat my yogurt?'

Using pictures

What you need
White cards (approximately 9 x 9cm) on which you draw pictures with 'deliberate mistakes', e.g., with things missing or with something wrong. For this age (rising-twos) the mistake must be very obvious and there should only be one mistake per card.

What you do
Show him one of the cards and ask: 'What's wrong with the picture? Is there something missing?' Help him if he can't do it first time round and then show him another card. If he still doesn't understand the activity, or is finding it too difficult, leave it and go back to it after a few weeks.

The missing toy

Line up some toys against a wall or on a table (about four to begin with). Look at them together for a while and talk about them: 'Look, I've put some of your toys here. Here's teddy, here's your ball, here's your red car and here's your book. If you close your eyes, one of your toys is going to hide. Close them tight and don't peep. All right, you can open them now. Can you tell me which toy is hiding?'

Jigsaw puzzles

Small children find jigsaw puzzles very difficult. It is probably best if you offer your child one or two that you have made yourself.

What you need
Stick a picture of a toy or household object from an old book or magazine onto a piece of white card. Cut the cards into half, thirds or quarters so that you have a two-, three-, or four-piece jigsaw:

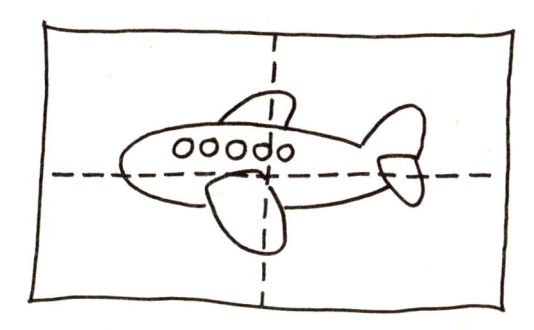

What you do
Sit down with your child with a two-piece jigsaw. Put the two pieces together and say: 'Look, this is a picture of a plane. Here is the nose (or front), here's the tail (or back) and here are the wings.' Move the two pieces apart and say: 'I'm going to put the picture back together now.' After two or three demonstrations, move the pieces apart and ask him: 'Can you put the picture back together?'

You can, of course, make lots of these jigsaws. If he finds them too easy then make a 'wavy' cut so that fitting the pieces together is slightly more difficult.

Some shops stock five-piece jigsaws, but even these will be cut in such a way that most under-twos find them too difficult. By all means try your child with one of these, but if it is obvious that it is too hard for him, show him how it is done and then put it away for a few weeks or even months.

Playtrays look very easy to adults and many children are given them as presents at far too young an age. Take care that you don't expect too much of your child with a seemingly easy puzzle, or you will put him off them for life!

CHAPTER 2
THE ADVENTUROUS INFANT – 2-3 YEARS

This is the age of the 'terrible twos', and a time of great mental as well as physical development. Your child will be able to climb, jump, stand on one leg, walk on tiptoe, backwards and sidewards, and will kick a ball hard and catch it between outstretched arms. His vocabulary will expand from tens of words put together in very short sentences to asking endless questions in longer sentences in muddled grammar.

At two, he explores mostly physically. At three he explores mentally as well as physically. He wants to know about everything: 'Why do you put gloves on to wash up, Mummy?', 'Daddy, why does smoke come out of the kettle?', 'Mummy, can I drive the car?' Some of the questions can be embarrassing, but you are going to have to be ready with an answer, because he won't give up: 'Mummy, is that man a giant?' (in a loud voice), and 'Mummy, are you old?' (in an even louder voice). Most of your time will be spent in coping with his questions, and in explaining how he can cope with various problems. He will begin to play more with other children and to understand that things have happened in the past as well as in the present. He will speak with more expression, copying you, the actors on television and other children.

At this age you should aim to develop:

• *The range of vocabulary* Because he is questioning so much this is not difficult, but you should remember to point out to him other things that he does not notice but that you consider important. The most obvious thing to point out at this age is the danger of cars and lorries on the road. A child of this age is also a wanderer and you should start training him early not to run out into the road.

• *His reading* Some children become ready to read at this age. It's true that they are in the minority but if your child is one of them he will derive great satisfaction and happiness from learning to read.

• *Certain mathematical ideas* There is no reason why some children should not be able to match, sort and order a few real objects by three years of age, though perhaps fewer will be able to pair objects as shown in this chapter. Counting should be extended as far as your child wants and using real objects. He may now be ready to recognize some numbers.

Your child will also begin to appreciate roundness, circle, triangle, rectangle, square, cube and sphere both through using sticky shapes, different-shaped blocks and objects shown to him in real life.

• *The range of creative activities* This will make sure that his desire to act out stories of fantasy and real life, his musical understanding and his need to express himself with brush, paint and pencil are all satisfied.

• *The range of investigative activities* Such activities will satisfy his need to know 'why?' This is really the beginning of science, and he will want to know *why* a kettle steams, *why* it snows, *why* ice melts, *why* bubbles happen in the bath, and so on.

• *The range of measuring activities* He is probably ready to start learning to measure and compare distances, weights and volumes.

Development: 2-3 years

- He can walk backwards and kick a ball well.
- He climbs furniture and pedals a tricycle.
- He can build bridges and high towers.
- He can cut with scissors after a bit of practice.
- He can write with a pencil as he gets nearer to three and draw recognizable pictures.
- He can use a knife and fork and will help you to do things around the house.
- He is learning to share things and to play with other children.

Talking

You should continue naming everyday objects as you did before he was two years of age, but now begin to talk as much with him about descriptive words like soft, close, open, hard, smooth, poor, dark, light, happy, sad, cross, melting, hot, cold, boiling, etc. At this age children are becoming more affectionate and communicative: they need to express their feelings and need words which will help them tell you what their feelings are.

He will talk to you in single words or short sentences, but by the age of three he may be talking relatively fluently and it is your job to encourage this and to give him the grammar to be able to put sentences together. However, don't criticize. If he expresses himself incorrectly, just respond with the correct form. For example, if he says, 'Me spill milk', you could say, 'Yes, I spill milk sometimes, too.' In other words, let him hear you speaking naturally and correctly.

Talk to him about his problems, too. There is such a vocabulary explosion at this age that you will spend much of your time not only naming objects, or even feelings, but explaining how he can eat his food without spilling it, why he should share his toys, why he should not run straight into the road without looking, etc.

Activities to provoke discussion

Using your ears

What you need
Objects that make sounds: keys, a whistle, clock, bell and so on.

What you do
Put these objects into a box or hat. Ask him to turn away, or close his eyes, and them make a sound with one of the objects. Ask him if he can describe the sound, and see if he can say what makes that sound and what it can be used for. Remember, though, this is really a conversation. If he does not know fairly quickly what the sound is, what makes the sound, what the objects are used for, then you should provide the explanation.

Using your eyes
This is a variation of 'I Spy'. Choose objects to describe and see if he can identify them. For example, you say: 'Let's play a game. I spy with my little eye (point to your own eye) something which is green (if he knows the colour), has one of these on it (hold up a leaf) and is in the garden.' If he can't guess that you are talking about a tree, help him and take him to the tree and show him everything that goes to make up what we call a tree: branches, leaves, trunk, bark, roots, etc.

Bricks, sorting and shapes

Building bridges with bricks

His ability to build bridges is an indication of his manipulative skills. First, show him how to build a simple bridge. Say: 'We need three bricks. I put one here, I put another one here, and this one goes on top to make the bridge. Can you do it?'

When he is finding this activity easy, suggest more complicated bridge building. Say: 'Why not build a harder bridge? Do it like this if you want to.' And show him one or two ways of building these bridges:

Leave him to experiment. If he finds this activity difficult, leave it and come back to it in a few weeks' time.

Building higher towers

As your child gets older he will be able to build higher and higher towers, and he will derive great satisfaction from doing this. Show him how to build a really high tower, and leave him to try it out for himself.

Sorting

Clothes

After the washing and ironing have been finished, ask your child to sort out various items of clothing. When he is very young, simply ask him to sort out and separate piles of socks, shirts, jumpers, pants. Help him at first by putting one of each in a different place and saying: 'Can you help me sort the washing out? Please put all the socks here, all the shirts here, all the jumpers here and all the pants here.' Once he can manage it easily then see if he can sort out each pile into light and dark groups. When he is older you might find that he can sort out and match pairs of socks.

Cards

You can teach your child the important mathematical principle of grouping by pairing pictures in games like Snap, Whist and Happy Families.

What you need
To make you own cards, cut out from a sheet of white cardboard ten cards about 15cm long and 10cm wide. Trace, draw or stick a picture onto the card. Then make another identical card, until you have the set of five pairs of cards.

What you do
Mix up the pairs into one pile and show him how to sort into pairs. Explain as you go along what the pictures are: for example, Mr Bun the Baker is the shopkeeper who makes bread and cakes. Explain to your child who he is and what he does and answer any questions that he asks. If the cards have words, point out each word and what it

says. This is a very popular game with small children and they come back to it many times over the years.

Crockery

What you need
In the beginning use plastic cups and paper plates, or buy a toy teaset (it will give good play value for some years to come).

What you do
Put two cups, two plates, two plastic knives and two plastic forks into a pile and, at first, say to your child: 'See if you can put these into piles of the same sort of thing.' If he can't do it at first, then show him. If he does it very quickly then increase the number of items or the number of cups, plates, knives and forks that he uses.

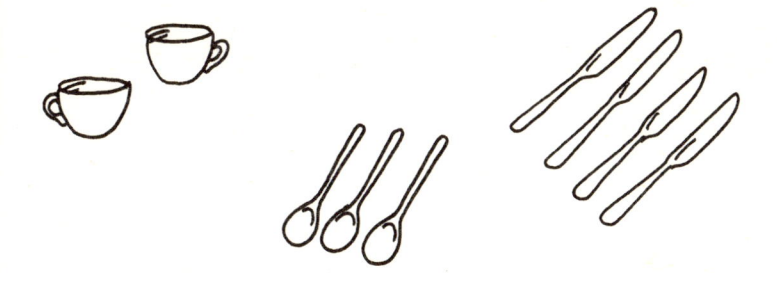

Don't worry if your child has some difficulty with sorting – this is usually an activity for at least a rising-three. Just be patient; keep showing him how and one day he will do it. Meanwhile, encourage him to help you set places at the table and to put away the cutlery after washing up.

Pairing

Some two-and-a-half-year-olds may be able to pair objects. Laying the table will help them with this, so that they know that cups go with saucers and knives go with forks. 'Pairing' teaches another important principle in mathematics when children learn that 3 + 5 = 8 or 5 + 3 = 8.

What you need
Equal groups of different objects, e.g., three cups, three saucers, three spoons, etc.

What you do
Put a small pile of three cups and three saucers on the table. Say to him: 'Put each cup on one saucer, like this.' Show him how to do it, then ask him to do the same. If he finds it too easy then increase the number of cups and saucers, or extend the game by introducing spoons as well.

At the end of the game, show him how to put three knives, forks, spoons, plates and cups away in their own place or pile in the cupboard or in the drawer.

Toys

Get your child to sort his toys into piles of books, cars, animals, dolls, trains, balls, etc. Use only two or three of each type to start with or he may find this too difficult.
   Make sure that there are separate boxes or compartments in the toy box, so that he can sort out his toys as he puts them away at night time. Say to him: 'Put your cars here, your books here, your dolls here.' Help him at the beginning. By three years of age he should be very good at sorting into appropriate groups.

Colours

This activity was begun at a younger age, but encourage your child to continue sorting by colour as well as by shape or size.

Shapes

Now is the time to start naming shapes as you carry on the activity from the last chapter.

Using sticky-paper shapes

Teach your child shapes one at a time. Try a circle shape to begin with. As you stick it onto the paper say: 'This is a circle shape. It is round.' When he is a little older you could write out the word circle in large lower-case letters and paste it onto a white card below a circle shape. Explain that round is also a ball shape: 'A ball is *round* as well as a circle', as you show him a ball. Ask him to find round things: oranges, grapefruit, marbles, bricks, bubbles. Help him *feel* the shape of roundness. Let him make patterns with circle shapes on a sheet of blank paper. Play circle games like 'Ring a ring o'roses'.

When you are sure that he understands about *circle* and *round* (it may be days, it may be weeks), introduce triangle. Stick a triangle shape onto a blank paper. Explain that it has three sides and count them out to him. See if there are any triangular shapes around the house, on the way to the Shops (for example, road signs). Get him to make patterns with a triangular shape – you can show him how.

Reading

Reading to your child

Reading to your two-and-a-half-year old is even more rewarding than reading to an eighteen-month-old child, because he will be much more interested. Now you can read longer stories because his attention span is that much greater. While you are still asking questions about pictures and about characters from the stories, *he* will now be asking *his own* questions and you will have to spend a lot of time answering them. Try not to say 'Not now, we have to finish the story.' This will stop him from asking questions in the end and will also reduce his interest in reading in general. At this age he must get used to talking around a picture as well as having the words read to him.

Poetry

Children at this age are very keen on rhymes and jingles, which they love to repeat. Now is also the time to start reading short poems. However, you must choose them carefully and your child should lead the way. Experiment with poems to see what holds his interest after a few bedtime repetitions. I found that *What is Pink?* by Christina Rossetti fascinated my children, but needed to be read with a lot of expression:

> What is pink?
> A rose is pink
> By the fountain's brink ...

Ask your local library for books of poems compiled specially for the under-fives. You should find an enormous selection, mostly well illustrated.

Riddles also fascinate children at this age. Make some up of your own, but keep them simple:

THE ADVENTUROUS INFANT – 2-3 YEARS

I have four legs.
I bark.
And I wag my tail.
Who am I?

I am big.
I have four wheels.
I carry a lot of people.
Who am I?

Riddle-me-ree,
You can toast me,
You can butter me,
And eat me for tea.
Who am I?

Pre-reading activities

Reading cards

You can now extend the reading card activities to cover not only objects that he can see round the house and in the street but also things that he can see on television and in books and magazines. Cut out or draw pictures to stick on the cards and write the word in lower-case lettering above or beneath the picture. Look out for picture books with one large word on the opposite page to the picture or below it (you may find them in jumble sales, fêtes, at your local bookshop or library).

The list of nouns that you can choose from is very extensive. Here are suggestion for some of the words for reading cards which should be found in reading books:

apple	banana	dog	mouse
tiger	bird	grass	garden
train	newspaper	man	child
ball	orange	cat	horse
lion	parrot	tree	house
car	book	plane (or	lady
girl	boy	aeroplane	letter
baby	bed	table	cup
fork	plate	postbox	window
football	fire	bicycle	shoes
hat	trousers	socks	pavement
bus	cake	shops	chair
knife	spoon	postman	door
flower	carpet	hand	foot
coat	gloves	dress	road
lorry	bus stop	bread	sweet

Make sure that you write all words in large clear letters.

When you show a picture and its accompanying word to your child, say the word clearly and go on to the next one. Don't present him with more than three or four words with accompanying pictures at any one time; go through these words with their pictures over a couple of weeks, and then move on to new ones. He won't tire of the repetition; on the contrary, he will like it. If you do find that he picks up the words presented with the pictures very quickly, then of course move on to new pictures much sooner.

Ready for reading

As you use the reading cards and picture books with accompanying words, there will come a time when your child will start to recognize words when the pictures are covered up. *It is essential that you do not try to push him into saying words on their own – this will only lead to a sense of failure and frustration on his part.* All reading work should be done in a relaxed and natural way and you must be patient. The range of readiness to read is very great indeed. Some children can recognize words as babies, others not until they are coming up to school age. Don't be disappointed if the signs of readiness to read are not there; simply continue with other pre-reading activity until the time comes. Above all, make sure he still sees reading and books as something to enjoy.

Choice of a reading scheme

There are various methods of teaching children to read. Two methods particularly prevalent at this time are 'look and say', and 'the sentence method'. Both will help your child to build up a limited vocabulary quite quickly, but later you may need to teach phonics (basic word sounds) so that your child can eventually read any word.

Look and say

For many children who can remember words easily this method gives quick success. When looking for a reading scheme choose one which is carefully graded; includes both real-life and imaginative and fairy stories; has flash cards (although, of course, you can make your own).

This is the system that I have used very successfully with my four children, although one child had a certain amount of difficulty in recalling some words and had to be helped with phonics.

There are certain disadvantages to using 'look and say'. I found that two of my children who were very ready to read at two years of age were learning words so quickly that after a couple of months they were using about seventy flash cards. Also, some reading schemes were beginning to bore the children after a few books; the best schemes had graded books with exciting fairy stories running alongside the main scheme. The best way to deal with this situation is to start on the main reading scheme for a short time as your child is able to cope with them. For some children the 'look and say' method can result in lack of fluency in reading. The reading schemes are partly to blame, as is reading one word at a time. However, I found that if a child is very ready to read, he will quickly go on to better written and more fluent styles after a successful early stage with 'look and say'.

What you need
- The first books of a reading scheme with large printed words and clear pictures. Make sure that the scheme uses large lower-case letters in the first book or two with few capitals. Each page should repeat words from the previous page, and occasionally add new words.
- Flash cards for the books.
- Exciting stories written at about the same word level as the reading scheme books. It is important to find good interesting stories which allow your child to systematically build up a memory bank of words.

What you do
The initial aim should be to stimulate your child's interest. So, make learning to read a game and a real pleasure. Just as when you read stories to him, work through the books for a few pages, pointing to the pictures and talking about them as you say the words. In the beginning, don't try to spell out the words to him but try to attract his interest in the situation or story. After a few days of working through the book you are ready to play a game with a few of the flash cards.

Flash card game
Say: 'We are going to play a game. These are some words

for your new book. I am going to say a few words to you. When I say each word I want you to say it after me, and when you have said it after me you can keep the card.' Each time he says the word, praise him – 'Well done', 'Good' – and give him the card. In the beginning, don't go very far in the book and don't use more than four or five flash cards. As you use the flash cards point out clues to starting letters. For example, the letter 's' has a snake shape, so a word beginning with 's' like *sweet* has a snake shape at the beginning. Emphasize the sound that the 's' makes. Also point out other patterns to words; man, for example, has the shape 'm' at the beginning and 'n' at the end. 'I' is like a tall, thin man standing straight up. It is important to emphasize shapes because a word is a shape, just as a circle is a shape, and if you give him some shapes to identify in the words, he will be able to look for those.

Exploring play

Water: floating and sinking

You should now extend the activities for under-twos to a game about floating and sinking. Whether or not you use bath-time, a sink half filled with water, a bowl of water or a paddling pool for this activity, you can introduce him to a guessing game about what will float and what will sink.

What you need
Various articles which will float and sink: for example, soap, metal toy, a wooden or plastic brick, marbles, matchsticks.

What you do
Take a metal toy and a matchstick. Put them in the water. Point out that one will float (emphasize the word) and the other will sink (emphasize the word). Now try him with each object in turn: 'Do you think this will float or sink?' After he has answered 'Yes', or 'No', or 'Don't know', let him try the object and see for himself what happens. 'Let's put it in the water and see. Does it float?'

Bubbles

Your child will love bathtime if you use some bubblebath. He can spend hours watching how bubbles behave, both in the water and in the air. Give him plastic cups and play containers so that he can investigate filling up and pouring from one container into another, just as you did in the previous chapter. Show him that when he pours from a small container into a large one he may have to fill up the small container several times before the large one can be completely filled.

Other finding-out activities

Heavier and lighter
Invest in a simple child's weighing balance:

It should be the kind which is supported in the centre and

has hands equidistant from the centre. You could also make a simple balance with a ruler and a piece of Plasticine.

First, shape the Plasticine to take the flat part of the ruler. Then rest the centre of the ruler on the centre of the Plasticine. Now your child can see which of his toys is the heaviest. This is a little difficult for a small child because he has first to learn how to balance the ruler before putting the toys on – you would have to help him. Try sticking the toys onto the ruler with a little Plasticine. Explain to him what you are going to do and how to do it. 'We are going to see how much your toys weigh. Let's start with your big marble and your blue car. You pick them up. Which one is heavier? The marble feels heavier does it? Let's put them on the scales and see. Put the marble here, and the car here. Which end has gone down? That's right, the end with your big glass marble on. Clever boy, you were right. Your marble is heavier than your plastic car.'

After he has weighed his toys show him how to line them all up in order – from the heaviest to the lightest. Point to the toys and as you point to them say: 'This is the heaviest', and go to the other end of the line and say, 'This is the lightest', then move along the line pointing to the toys and saying in turn, 'This toy is heavier than this toy, and this toy is heavier than this toy', all the way along until you get to the lightest one.

Blowing through a straw

Show your child how to blow through a straw. Ask him to put his finger or palm near the end so that he can feel the air coming out. Show him that blowing air through a straw can move bits of paper, ruffle hair, make water ripple and feels cold to the touch. Play racing games with straws and ping-pong balls or balloons.

Explain that air is all around us and that when he blows through a straw it has a lot of *push*. If you think he can understand, explain a little about the air coming out of our mouth from the inside of our chest (but don't explain too much at this age).

Hands

Talk to your child about his hands: how many fingers has he got? What are they used for? Explain and demonstrate words like 'push', 'pull', 'hold', 'point', 'slap', 'pick-up'.

Eyes

Explain that we use our eyes for seeing; point out the different colours of eyes, point out the colour of his eyes, using a mirror; point out the colour of your eyes. Ask him to close one eye: 'Can you see as much now?'
own work: black, white, red, yellow, blue. By mixing these the paper. Make it all very enjoyable. When you are sure

Ears

Explain that these are used for hearing. Ask him what happens when he puts his hands over his ears.

Feeling things

What you need
A cloth, orange, apple, spoon, brick, toy car, piece of fur.

What you do
Put two objects into a box and ask him to say what each of these feels like in turn, without looking. After he has explained what the object feels like he may be able to say what it is. He will need to use words like 'rough', 'soft', 'smooth', 'cold', 'warm', etc, to describe what he is feeling.

Reflections
Ask him to look into a mirror: 'What can you see? Move away from the mirror: what can you see now?' What happens when he moves towards the mirror?

Dissection
Cut open an apple. Show him what is inside. Talk about the pips, peel, stalk, skin. Do the same with a pear. Explain that the apple falls off an apple tree, and in the end the pips go into the ground and grow into a new tree. Plant a pip (an avocado pip is easiest) and watch it grow.

Creative play

Drawing and painting

Painting

You can extend your child's painting by teaching him to use a paint brush. If, however, he finds great difficulty in handling a brush, then leave him with finger painting for at least a few more weeks. By three, however, he should be able to hold a brush quite well. (Choose a thick brush with a short handle. If necessary you can cut down a long one.)

Mix up these basic colours and leave him to create his own work: black, white, yellow, blue. By mixing these colours together he can make all the others. Make certain that he has his painting clothes on and that there is a double layer of newspaper on the table.

Drawing

When he gets to two-and-half years of age you can start trying him with a pencil. Put a large sheet of white cartridge paper on the table and show him how to hold a pencil to draw lines, circles and other squiggly shapes on the paper. Make it all very enjoyable. What you are sure that he can use the pencil well, leave him to experiment. Coloured pencils are best for creative drawing and you can also let him use the fat crayons he used before he was two. Useful colours for crayons and pencils are: red, orange, green, yellow, blue, purple, pink, black, grey.

Always hang his painting or drawings up in some prominent place when he has finished them. This adds to his pride and satisfaction in his own work.

Using scissors

For safety choose plastic scissors with blunt ends. Put some old newspaper on the table and show him how to cut through the paper. Don't show him how to cut round things yet; just leave him to enjoy himself. But please do make sure that he knows that he mustn't cut up today's newspaper, or the curtains, or anything to which he takes a fancy.

Acting

Making faces
When you are reading fairy stories, ask your child to make the faces of the giant, or Jack, to show how he is feeling at a particular point. Ask: 'How does the giant feel? Sad? Happy? Can you make a sad face? That's very good. Now, can you make a happy face?' If he can't show you very easily, then you must show how at first.

Playing a part
Occasionally get him to play a part from a story you have read together and you can join in with him. For example, he can be Little Billy-Goat-Gruff and you can be Big Billy-Goat-Gruff, or he can be one of the little pigs in the three little pigs, and you can be the wolf. This really is great fun for him but be careful that you don't let the acting replace a pure reading to your child. Just try this activity from time to time, or when your child asks for it.

Dancing

Don't forget to provide your child from time to time with music he can dance to. Switch on the record player or cassette player or radio and suggest that he has a dance. This is a marvellous age for dancing as the children will have wonderful few inhibitions about dancing freely.

Music

Game one
At this age your child is ready to respond to a 'stop/start' signal.

Sit him down with pots, pans, toy xylophone, toy drum, toy whistle, and other things that make sounds. Tell him to start playing when you bang a ruler on the floor or table in front of him, and to stop when you bang again. At the beginning you may have to say 'Start now', or 'Begin', or 'Stop now', or 'Finish', as well as bang the ruler.

Game two: musical statues
Your child can play this game on his own or with other children. It will help him to connect movement and dancing with music, and follows up the 'stop/start' signal learned in game one. Tell him very clearly what you want him to do. Say: 'when the music plays you can start dancing, but you must stop when the music stops.' You may have to remind him about this as the game goes on.

Have a variety of music to dance to, either on record or tape, children's songs, waltzes, jazz and pop.

Game three
This will help him to understand loud and quiet and also getting louder and quieter.

Get him to play loud and quiet on his 'band'. Emphasize the word by saying, 'Play *loud* now'. If he is not sure what to do, then show him. Later you should be able to get him to vary the noise level by saying, 'Now play *quieter*', or 'Now play much *louder*'. If he is not sure what to do, then show him very clearly, emphasizing the word as you do it, 'Louder', 'Quieter'. Adapt the song 'I can do anthing better than you can' from *Annie Get Your Gun* to 'I can sing anything louder/quieter than you can'.

Game four
Sing a children's song to him in a high voice and then in a low voice. Say to him: 'I am going to sing high now', and afterwards, 'See if you can sing high as well'. Later on you may be able to introduce the idea of lower and higher.

Favourite songs
Even at this age you should be able to teach him some simple songs, and some two-and-a-half-year-olds can sing in perfect key.

Here is a list of simple songs that may be useful:

- Twinkle, twinkle, little star
- Skip to my Lou
- Away in a manager
- It's raining, it's pouring
- Diddle, diddle dumpling
- Jingle bells
- The animals went in two by two
- Rat a tat tat
- The wheels on the bus go round and round

You can reinforce the beat as you sing together by tapping a ruler on the table or the floor, or clapping your hands.

Clapping songs
- If you're happy and you know it clap your hands
                                     stamp your feet
                                     laugh out loud
                                     shout 'hurrah'
- A sailor went to sea, sea, sea

Again, for a wider repertoire, borrow tapes, records or books from your library.

Counting extension

With buttons

Extend your child's counting as far as he wants to go. Count different but real things. Buttons are very useful, especially as he begins to want to count further and further. Make sure that you sit up at the table with him on your knee and lay out the buttons in front of you to count. Count in stages. First he learns how to count up to five (five fingers, five coins, five pencils five buttons, five cakes, five matchsticks, five spoons); then you teach him how to count to ten. After that you can help him to count up to twenty, and it won't be very long before he's counting up to 100. All you have to do is to stand by and answer his questions: 'Mummy, what comes after twenty-nine? Is it twenty-ten?'

With an abacus

A children's abacus can also be useful for counting. Count with him as far as he wants to go; he should find it a pleasure, and you can tell if he is enjoying it because he will keep asking 'What is the next one?' It may help if you have an abacus which has ten rows of ten beads. It is certainly much easier than having to lay out 100 buttons!

Counting rhymes

For example:
>One, two, buckle my shoe.
>Three, four, knock at the door.
>Five, six, pick up sticks.
>Seven, eight, open the gate.
>Nine, ten, a big, fat hen.

>Five green bottles a-hanging on the wall (*repeat twice*)
>If one green bottle should accidentally fall,
>There'd be four green bottles a-hanging on the wall.

One man went to mow, went to mow a meadow.
One man and his dog
Went to mow a meadow.

'Five green bottles' is a take-away or subtraction rhyme. If you replace the bottles with rabbits you can reverse the song and then you have an adding or addition rhyme, e.g., 'One furry rabbit sitting on a hill, along came another one and then there were two', etc.

Games

Snakes and Ladders
Introduce him to games like Snakes and Ladders when he can count reasonably well. This is one of the best games for extending counting but you will need to explain about counting in different directions on different rows of the Snakes and Ladders board. All the struggle will be worth it though if the game gives much pleasure. Snakes and Ladders is also a good introduction to written numbers.

Dominoes
Dominoes is another game to start him on at this age, but when you choose a set make sure that the dots on the individual dominoes are very large and clear, otherwise he is likely to get confused.

Introducing numbers

Cut out ten pieces of card about 7 x 7 cm. Write the numbers clearly on each card with the corresponding number of dots beneath each number.

Show your child one card at a time. Get him to count the dots and say the numbers with you. Do the numbers from one to five only until he is really sure of them. Then do the numbers up to ten. You may find that your child likes to count his fingers as well as to count the dots. Don't stop him from doing this because for him it's an added enjoyment.

Measurement

From a very young age you can measure your child's height (in centimetres) and mark it on the wall. Compare his height with other children's, and as the years go on he can see how his height increases and how his brother's and sister's and friend's heights increase.

When John was this age I made a metre stick in card for him to use in measuring outside in the garden, along the path and in the long front living-room.

Problem-solving

Puzzles

Many three-year-olds can complete nine-piece jigsaw puzzles and so you can feel fairly safe in trying a two-and-a-half-year-old with a four- or five-piece puzzle. However, if it does become obvious that your child will not be able to complete a puzzle fairly quickly, put it away for a few weeks.

With all the activities the emphasis should be on enjoyment, a short struggle with the problem and a successful solution.

CHAPTER 3
THE AGILE INFANT – 3-4 YEARS

At three years of age your child is becoming physically very agile and will be climbing over the furniture and trying to climb the garden trees. He will be able to kick, bounce and throw a ball. He will learn to dress himself. He will be questioning everything and even be trying to tell *you* how much he knows.

Most children of this age are able to learn to write, some will be ready to read and a large number will be capable of doing what many parents call 'sums', though these will be very simple sums. This is the age when reading, writing and arithmetic will be learned for the first time. It will be your job to help your child learn these skills through games, *but only* if he wants to, and at his own pace.

Development: 3-4 years

- Can be taught to cut along a line with scissors. Will learn

to catch, throw and kick a ball, and play cricket.
- He can draw a cross and can be taught to write some letters.
- He draws a man with a head, body, arms and legs.
- He can wash and dress himself, and he uses a knife and fork at table.

Choosing a nursery school

By this age your child will be old enough to start nursery school. Most nursery schools provide facilities for children to paint, play with Plasticine or toys, and devote some time to singing and learning rhymes and jingles. However, any good nursery school will also provide for the needs of the individual. It should cater for those children who are beginning to read and write and are starting to do sums.

Take your child to the local nursery school and ask them what they can offer him. If they insist that he will just have to fit into a rigid scheme, then you might as well assume that they will not be able to meet your child's mental needs, and that he is likely to be bored rather than stimulated.

Do try to find a good nursery school for him though, because he is at the stage where he needs to socialize with children of his own age. He also needs to learn to spend time away from home and how to communicate with other adults.

Sunday school

Don't dismiss Sunday school as a waste of time. Some Sunday school teachers work hard to make that one hour a week very interesting for the children. They often provide good, creative, dramatic and musical activities for small children.

Talking

Your child is now coming up to four years of age and his actions add real meaning to words like 'run', 'jump', 'twist', 'skip', 'hop', 'bounce', 'throw', 'ride', 'climbing', 'hit', and many other verbs that describe his exuberant behaviour. Take advantage of all the new things he is learning to do and talk about them. As you talk to him, turn his inventive expressions and sentences into the correct ones. So when he says, 'Yesterday I get very wet', you say, 'Yes, yesterday you got very wet, didn't you?' Respond naturally but correctly. The worst thing you can do is to stop him experimenting with words and sentences.

By now his learning and vocabulary will be so well developed that he will really enjoy lots of word games, riddles and puns. Games like 'Finishing off the nursery rhyme' (p.91) and 'Rhyming words' (p.92) will not only give him a chance to play with his ever-developing language skill but prepare him for early phonic work.

Mathematics

Now is the age when you will be able to greatly extend the discovery of mathematics.

Matching

Colours
This is really an extension of what you did at the two to three age. You can use colour cards, coloured bricks or any objects about the house or garden.
   Ask him to match colours as, for example, you sort the washing: 'Can you put all the blue clothes in the corner?';

'Put all the red socks on the table so we can see which ones go together'; 'Can you put all the brown Smarties together? They're the ones Daddy likes best', etc.

Length

Bricks Together, sort out nine bricks which are all the same size. Explain that you want to make three trains all the same length and arrange the bricks in sets of three side-by-side. Point out that they are all the same length – they are all three bricks long. 'Can you see?' They are all as long as each other. They have all got three bricks (or an engine and two carriages). Next take one brick away from one train, and two from another. See if he can show you which is longest now, which is the shortest. Ask him to make them all the same length again. Do this several times.

Straws. Take three straws and put them down on the table. Say, 'These straws are all as long as each other. Can you see what I mean? If he is not clear about the words 'as long as', hold the straws between the palms of your hand to show him they are the same length.

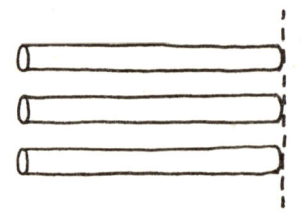

Next, cut the straws to different lengths. Now you can use words like 'longer than', and 'shorter than'.

Shapes

Use bricks and flat shapes to show size and shape. Show him a variety of shapes and bricks which are the same shape and size, e.g., large and small cuboids, large and small triangles. Then mix up the shapes and bricks and ask him to put them in groups of the *same shape and size.*

Cards

Make sets of cards that can be matched for either the same picture or the same colour or the same shape. Make sure that each pair is identical so that he won't be confused. Then ask him to match them *either* by picture *or* by colour *or* by shape.

Sorting letters from numbers

What you need
Make some cardboard cut-outs of about five numbers and five letters that he knows well (make sure the letters are lower case letters).

What to do
Put letters and numbers into a pile on the table. Say to him: 'I want you to put numbers in this pile, and letters in this pile!' Show him how to sort numbers from letters, then jumble them up and ask him if he can do it. If he cannot do it the first time, show him again.

Pairing

Prop three dolls or teddy bears up against the wall, or sit them on chairs. Count out loud as you do it: 'Let's put the teddies against the wall like this: one teddy, two teddies, three teddies. Lay three sweets out in front of your child, again, counting as you do so. Ask him: 'Are there enough sweets for each teddy?' If he says 'No', show him that each teddy can have one sweet and there will be none left over. Ask him to give each teddy a sweet. Play this game several times with different objects, e.g., marbles to go into lorries or playcups, drinks for the family, cakes for his friends etc., each time making sure that there are equal numbers.

Ordering with straws

Make patterns like those shown opposite. Explain as you do it: 'Look, I'm making a pattern. One short straw, then one long straw, a short straw then a long straw. What comes next?' or 'Two short straws, one long straw, two short straws. What comes next?'

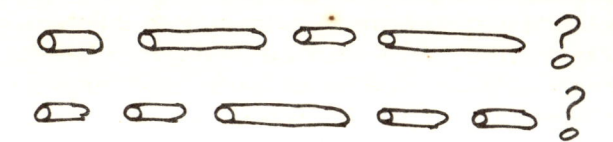

Try different variations.

With shapes
As above explain what you are doing. 'I'm making a pattern with these bricks. First a cone, then a sphere, then a cube; a cone; a sphere – what comes next?'

Try other variations. Most children of this age will be able to do only the simplest ordering.

With toys

What you need
Pencils and toys of different lengths.

What you do
Say: 'Put your pencils on the table in a row. Start with the shortest and finish with the longest.' When he has finished that, say: 'Now put them in order from the longest to the shortest.' When he has finished this activity, see if he can do the same with the toys.

Counting

You can go to town now on extending his counting, because if you have followed the activities in the previous chapter, he should be very anxious to learn and count more and more.

When you next go to the supermarket, see if he can count the tins of beans or the packets of cornflakes as you go round. See if he can count cars as you walk along the street going to the shops; the number of people you pass as you go to the shops; birds in the sky as you walk along the street; houses in your road.

Numbers

Now he is counting more fluently, go over matching numbers of objects with number symbols. Using the number cards you made for the previous stage (see p.73), play lots of games where he has to match number symbols with the same number of objects. Start with the numbers 1 to 5 to begin with. Here are a few suggestions:

Buttons
Put the number cards 1 to 5 on the table. Ask him to put the right number of buttons by each card.

Sweets
Put out five groups of Smarties (or crisps or peanuts) as shown below. Ask him to put the right number card by each group. If he gets it right he can eat the sweets.

Fingers
Hold up different numbers of fingers. First ask him to tell you how many fingers you are holding up (you can count them together if necessary); then ask him to find the card with the right number on.

Once he is confident about playing these games with numbers 1 to 5, introduce the numbers 6 to 10 and then play them all over again.

Money

Shopping (for a rising-four)

What you need
A till; objects marked with prices; several coins of varying denominations (real, plastic or cardboard). (If he is still not sure of the value of the larger coins, then play shopping with only the lowest value coins.)

What to do
Set up the till on a table. Make sure you have several objects which are marked with prices, there is no need to mark the objects with the real shop prices. You can mark them at any low price which is not more than 5p for each. Then take it in turns to be the shopkeeper and the customer. As you each buy or take payment for something, count out clearly the number of coins which are handed over.

Beginning of addition

Using four bricks

What you need
Four wooden bricks.

What to do
Put one brick on the floor and say: 'Here is one brick'. Then put another brick on top of the first brick and say: 'Here is another brick. One brick and one more brick makes two.'

Finally say, 'One add one makes two', pointing to the bricks in turn. Repeat this activity several times. Now say to him: 'I have two bricks here. If I add one more brick to those two bricks how many bricks have I?' and put another brick on top. If he can't answer straightaway, tell him the answer and say: 'Two bricks, add one more brick makes three bricks. Two add one makes three', point to the two bricks and the one brick.

Play this game for a few days and then, if he is very clear about what is happening, go on to four bricks. You can say then: 'Three add one is four; two add two is four, two add one, add one is four; and one add one, add one, add one is four.'

Using fingers
You can show him how to do the same adding sums in his fingers:

Show him how one add one is two, holding up the index finger on the left and the right hand.

Using buttons
Sit up at the table with him and put the buttons in front of him. Take the buttons as you say 'one add one', then push the buttons together and say, 'makes two'.

1 + 1 = 2

He can now try the same adding activities as he did on his fingers using the buttons.

Addition cards
Make your own addition cards. Cut out rectangular pieces of card and on them draw pictures.

one pig
1

two pigs
2

Show him how to do the adding sums by pushing the cards together, and saying 'one pig add two pigs makes three pigs: one add two makes three.'

1 + 2 = 3

More than
Using addition cards and real objects you can show:

two is one more than one

three is two more than one

Beginning of subtraction

Using buttons
Sit your child at the table and put three buttons in front of him. Say to him: 'Here are one, two, three buttons. I am going to take one of the buttons away. How many are there left?' When he has told you that there are two left then say, 'That means that three take away one leaves two'. Try a few examples with him, showing him what to do and telling him the answer if he is not sure. Repeat the activity for a few days, or even a few weeks, but only spend a short amount of time on it. You could also change the buttons for toys or matchsticks or marbles or various other objects

from around the house. Play with sweets or biscuits where the taking away includes eating!

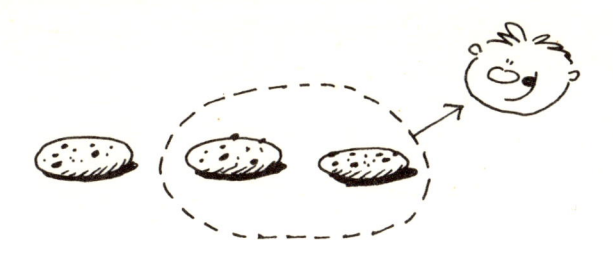

Using fingers
Hold up your left hand with three fingers sticking up, count each finger in turn, say 'one, two, three'. 'Here are three fingers. Now I am going to take one away?' Put down one of the three fingers and say to him, 'How many fingers have I left?' After he has given you the answer say, 'That means that three take away one leaves two.'

Zero (0)
Don't forget when you are doing the taking away activities to include an example where three take away three is zero. Explain that zero means that there are no apples, or spoons, or buttons, or fingers left.

Counting rhymes
These can be used to teach adding or taking away. For adding:
>One teddy bear sitting on the chair
>Add one more and
>*Two* teddy bears sitting on the chair
>Add one more and
>*Three* teddy bears sitting on the chair.

For taking away:
>Three teddy bears sitting on the chair
>Take one away and
>*Two* teddy bears sitting on the chair
>Take one away and
>*One* teddy bear sitting on the chair
>Take one away and
>*No* teddy bears sitting on the chair.

Use real teddies or other toys as you say the rhyme. Ask your child to add or take away the teddies.

Shapes: more words
Using bricks you can teach your child the names of the parts of different shapes.

Measuring

Length
You can measure distances around the room and show your child how to do it using:
• hand spans (the distance from thumb to small finger when fingers are spread).

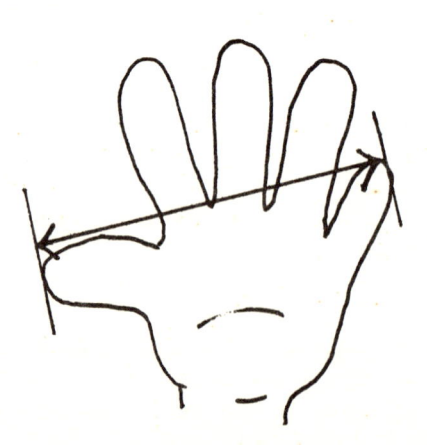

- Using feet.

- Using steps.

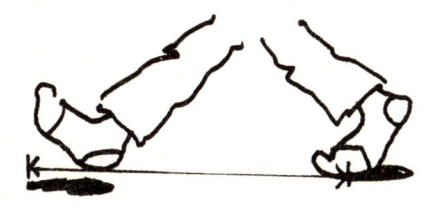

- Using a metre stick.

You can make a metre stick by using a tape measure to measure out exactly 100 cm on a large piece of cardboard. (Use the cardboard from a large box.) At this stage you don't need to mark off the metre stick into centimetres.

Using hand spans, foot distances, steps and a metre stick, encourage your child to measure distances in the downstairs rooms, bedroom, along the hall, outside along the path, in the back garden, in the front garden; get him to measure the heights of doors, the width of the carpet, length of the carpet. Get him used to the idea of 'measuring *about*' (whole numbers).

Volume
In the sink or in the bath he can play games using jugs and cups and mugs. By now you can start to ask him: about how many cups will it take to fill the big containers?' Which container holds the most?'

Weight

Now is the time to extend the activities that you were doing for the two-to three-year range. A good example would be to use marbles for weighing: a toy car weighs about two marbles; a small teddy bear weighs much more than ten marbles; a spoon weighs about four marbles.

A note on maths development

Some children are capable of much more advanced activities than those set out here. If your child learns very quickly and is always eager for more; then move on to the activities shown in Chapter 4.

Reading

Reading to your child

Now you can read longer stories to your child. He will begin to enjoy slightly more complex plots and savour new words, even if he isn't sure what they mean. His memory is good, his speech is well developed so now is the time to play the following game. When you have finished reading him a story, say to him: 'Now I want you to tell me about the story: what was it all about?' Let him describe the various incidents in the story as he remembers them. Encourage him to act out various parts of the story as he tells it. Help him out if he mimes or does actions to explain the various parts.

By this age there may well be favourite stories he knows by heart. He will enjoy 'reading' them to you and may even be able to pick out words and phrases which are repeated throughout the story.

Activities like these will add to his enjoyment of the richness of storytelling and keep his interest alive.

He may also enjoy re-enacting parts of films seen on television or video: Walt Disney's *Alice in Wonderland*, *The Water Babies*, or *The Wizard of Oz* are much-loved examples.

Nursery rhymes

By now he should know several nursery rhymes well enough to enjoy playing the following game.

What you need
Something that will make a noise – for example, a bell or a toy xylophone.

What you do
Pick out a favourite nursery rhyme or song, and when you come to the end of a line ring the bell instead of saying the final word:

This little piggy went to . . . (bell)
This little piggy stayed at . . . (bell)

Wait after the bell to see if your child can supply the missing word. If he can't do it quickly, then tell him what the answer is.

Rhyming words

At this age your child will probably know quite a few rhyming words, especially if he is used to hearing and repeating nursery and simple action rhymes. Games with rhyming words will help develop his ear and provide a good beginning for early phonics work. If he enjoys games, play a variation of 'I Spy' with him in which he has to find an object which sounds like another: for example 'I spy with my little eye something which sounds like "bog" ' (dog).

What you need
Picture cards or actual objects around the house.

What you do
Show the picture card or object to your child and see if he can find a word to rhyme with it. For example, if you show a clock, he could say 'lock' or 'rock'. If he finds the game difficult, don't spend any more time on it, but wait for a few weeks until he is ready for this activity.

Pre-reading activities

The best practice for reading is reading itself. There are forty-four basic sounds from which *all* words in the English language can be built up, but most children pick up these sounds through reading and more reading and through conversation with older children and adults. Two of my children learnt to read at two years of age.

One learnt sounds through phonics work (John) but the other 'picked up the sounds' through talking and reading over several months. It seemed to me that learning word sounds by simply reading was the more natural process. *If you wish to teach phonics, then you must take great care that your child enjoys what he is doing.*

Teaching phonics

Game one
Choose a consonant (for example 'c'), and say a sound the letter says – for example, 'c' for cat (use lower-case letters

always). Find several words that begin with 'c' consonant; car, cat, cap, cup, cot. You could draw pictures on card, or collect the objects. It is best to choose three-letter words. Leave these objects or cards in a corner for a few days, together with the white card, and come back daily to talk about them. Say: 'Tell me what these things are?' Point out that each of the objects begins with the letter 'c'. Show him everyday things which begin with 'c' – with the 'c' sound – cornflakes, for example. Play games like 'I spy with my little eye, something beginning with "c" '; or 'I'm thinking of an animal that begins with "c". It has four legs and goes "miaow".' When you feel sure that he knows this sound, introduce another consonant – 'p' and 't', for example.

p pin pen pan pot
t tin top tap

Game two
After your child knows a few consonants like this you can build up some simple words.

What you need
Separate cards for each letter of the alphabet ('q' should be written as 'qu').

What to do
Sit down with your child and start to build up words to go with the objects or pictures, For example, put down 'c' and ask him what it says. Then, alongside, put down 'u' and ask him what the letter is. If he doesn't know, don't worry but just tell him before putting down 'p'. See if he knows what the word is now. If he is not sure, then tell him straightaway.

This simplest form of word building and at this age it is best if you spend a lot of your phonic teaching time on three-letter words built up from learning single letter sounds. Some simple words that can be broken up this way are: can, cap, cat, cab, bag, dog, gun, bus, hat, net, van, jug, dot, box, hut, man, mop, bed.

Game three
When he knows some words which are built up in this

way, you can make up some sentences. For example, if he knows 'd', 'a', 'h', 's', 'o', 'g', then the sentence could be 'dad has a dog'.

Don't worry about capitals at this point. You can also link this activity with writing as explained later on in this section.

Continue with single letter sounds and building three-letter words for some time. You will come up against difficulties, particularly certain vowel sounds which are similar (for example, 'i' as in pit and 'e' as in pet). Remember, phonics is just an aid to reading. Your main way of teaching should be reading itself.

Reading with your child

You may be at the stage now where you are teaching your child either by 'look and say' with flash cards or perhaps the sentence method. You may be helping him build simple words by teaching him the sounds of the letters. However, by far the most important element is your involvement with his reading from his reading book. You can either sit with him up at a table and read his book with him, have him on your lap as he reads, or sit on the bed at bedtime and hear him read there. However you hear him read, you must be able to run your finger underneath the words. As you point to a word, he reads it out to you. If he does not say it quickly, say the first letter of the word. Then if he still does not respond quickly say the word and ask him to repeat it. Too many parents wait far too long for their child to say a word and a stressful relationship then begins to develop. Please remember not to make any reading session longer than about ten minutes (unless he is *very* keen) and try to hear him read at least once a day. This is the key to all early learning: daily repetition for a very short time. Many parents hear their child read one day then leave it until the next week, by which time he has forgotten all that he has learnt.

If he begins to struggle with his reading, try reading one page yourself, then let him read, or try to read, the next page. Or you could each read a sentence at a time.

Don't discourage guessing. It is a very useful way of learning words. If his guess is wrong say, 'Good guess' and immediately tell him the right word. Finally, continue with other good reading habits — that is, discuss the pictures, the characters, the events and the words themselves. It all helps to keep your child's interest alive and to help him become an active questioning reader who wants to make sense of what he is reading rather than just 'bark at the print'. Above all, keep reading to him from as wide a range of interesting books – fact and fiction – as possible.

Finding out activities

His immediate environment

In the beginning concentrate on his immediate environment: your home, your street, village or town. Show him buildings that are very old – some will have the date on them. If, for example, you see a building dated 1852 you could say: 'That was built even before Grandad was alive.' Take him to the local church and show him the stained-glass windows and the old arches. Talk about how old all these things are. Tell him when the houses in your street were built. Perhaps they are not even as old as him.

At the local library you may be able to get a map of your area. Try to explain what it means. Take him outside and show him the roads which are on the map, pick out landmarks that he knows – for example, a hill, the church, the centre of the village, a river, fair, or a school. Develop his interest in local history and geography.

Take him into the garden and talk to him about the plants, the trees, the sun, the moon and the stars. Take him down to the riverbank and talk about what lives in the river. Take him to town, the market, and talk about what is there. At this age he will learn far more from talking to you about real things than from books.

Television

Don't forget to select television programmes that will interest and also educate him. There are excellent pre-school and early school programmes: the ones he will probably like best are those that teach early reading skills, and sing-a-long music programmes for infants.

Pets

If you have a pet, talk to your child about it. Ask how many legs it has, how its body differs from ours, what it eats, what sounds it makes. Point out to your child the ways in which his pet resembles him, and the ways in which it differs from him.

Draw a picture of his pet on a large sheet of paper and get him to tell you what the names of the various parts of its body are. If he is not sure then tell him. Ask him what it would be like to be a cat, dog or a fish. Perhaps he could try drawing his own picture of his pet in paint or crayon.

Set up a bird table in the garden and let him watch the different birds that use it. Ask him to describe what they are like.

Take him to the zoo, or a local pet shop, so that he can see in the flesh animals he may only have seen in books or on the television.

Creative play

Painting

Continue the activities from the previous chapters encouraging your child to use brushes and fingers. Introduce using a sponge so your child can make pictures on large sheets of paper. Always talk to him about his picture and don't forget to praise him before you put it up on the wall for everybody to see.

Drawing and colouring

The emphasis here should be on free drawing and colouring, but he might like to try and copy the pictures in his story books or rhyme books. Real-life objects are best – a bus, a car, a house, a flower, a shop, a man, a lady, and so on. When he has finished his drawing, praise it generously whether or not it is like the original.

Cutting out with scissors

Now is the age when your child will begin to use scissors to cut along a straight line. Buy some large sheets of coloured sticky paper. Draw shapes with straight edges (for example, triangles, squares) on the backs of the sticky paper, and show him how to make pictures by sticking these on white paper or large squared graph paper. then leave him to experiment.

When he comes proficient at cutting out with scissors, show him how to cut out pictures from old catalogues, magazines or comics. He can then stick these onto a sheet of blank paper or into a scrap book using paste or glue. Before you start, ensure that there are two layers of newspaper on the table.

Making a collage

What you need
Coloured sweet wrappers, old cheap stamps, bits of coloured cloth, leaves, string, bits of magazines and a pot of paste or glue.

What you do
Spread a double layer of newspaper on the table. Show your child how to stick the various bits and pieces onto a large sheet of blank paper. Say: 'We are trying to make a pretty picture or a nice pattern.' Then leave him to carry on or give him a completely clean sheet of blank paper and leave him to experiment. (Make sure that he has got his painting overalls on otherwise the glue will get all over his best jumper.)

Plasticine

Put a wooden board or tray on the table and demonstrate how to make men, cars, boats, cakes, plates, houses, trees, flowers, etc. Then ask: 'Is there anything else that you would like us to make?' If there is, then continue in your role of demonstrator. If not, leave him to experiment.

Music

Listening to music
Now is the time to start developing your child's 'musical ear'. Let him hear a wide variety of music, from pop to jazz, from musicals to children's rhymes and songs, from classical to choral music. Ask him what he likes – you may be surprised. Here are some examples of music my children liked at this age:

- Children's songs in particular
- Some tuneful pop songs and other songs (for example, Elvis Presley's 'Wooden Heart' and 'Teddy Bear')
- Songs from the full length Disney cartoons (for example, *Snow White, Jungle Book, Pinocchio*)
- Some brass band music for example, '76 Trombones' from *The Music Man*)
- Some classical music (for example, 'Mars: the Bringer of War' from *The Planet Suite* by Holst, and 'Dance of the Sugar Plum Fairy' from *The Nutcracker* by Tchaikovsky).

Learning to play an instrument

If you have a piano or recorder in the house allow your child to make up his own 'tunes' on them. If he is very precocious musically you will soon notice.

A music game

You can help your child to develop a sense of pitch by playing notes on the piano. Use only middle C, D, E, F, G. These you can call doh, ray, me, fah, so (singing names) as well as their playing names. Make up a little tune of three notes and see if he can do the same – he may prefer to sing it out. Play this game regularly and when he improves sufficiently, increase the number of notes to an octave (C to C or Doh to Doh).

Two songs which are very useful within these ranges are: 'Twinkle, twinkle little star' and 'Lavender's Blue'. You might try the first line of one of these songs, for example, 'Twinkle, twinkle little star' and see if your child can learn it. For a child of nearly four who has a good musical sense, learning simple tunes like this can be very rewarding.

Some songs to sing

Here are the titles of some songs that children of this age like to sing:
- Pease pudding hot
- There was an old woman who swallowed a fly
- Hickory, dickory, dock
- It's raining, it's pouring
- Lavender's Blue
- Do you know the Muffin Man?

- Old MacDonald had a farm
- We all live in a yellow submarine

There are many, many more so your child should never lack for a good song to sing and dance to.

Acting and dressing-up

Don't forget to get out the dressing-up box from time to time, and especially when your child's friends come around to play.

Starting to write

Making patterns

Long before small children attempt to copy letter shapes, they need to practise controlling a pencil and the marks they make with it. When he was younger your child probably held the pencil (or wax crayon) in his fist and made large sweeping movements across the paper. By this stage he may well be able to hold the pencil in his fingers (do check that he starts off by holding it reasonably correctly) and is beginning to be able to control it well enough to make quite small regular movements. When he has reached this stage, give him a large sheet of blank paper and show him how to make patterns on it.

The simple patterns given opposite form the basic shapes needed to make most letters. Make sure that he sees how you make the patterns. Talk to him as you do so, explaining that you start on the left-hand side of the pattern and work from left to right, trying to keep the pencil in constant contact with the paper.

Tracing letters

Make some very large lower-case letters out of cardboard, Plasticine or sandpaper. Let your child trace over them with his finger, following the pattern needed to form the letter correctly, so that he can really feel the shape of the letter. Show him how to draw the letter in his sandtray, or in the air.

When he knows how to form the letters correctly, put some dotted letters onto paper and let him go over the dots in pencil. Make sure he is forming the letters correctly.

Writing his name

You can either write your child's name on a piece of paper and let him copy it or you can do his name in dots and let him go over it. The best thing is to try both methods. Don't press him too much with his writing, because he finds it hard work. Later on you can introduce him to his surname as well, and if he gets on with that very well, let him try to copy his address.

His first book

What you need
Four large rectangular sheets of blank paper, all the same size. Thick, white paper is the best.

What you do
Fold the paper down the middle so that you make a book; don't join the sheets together at this stage. On the front page you can write 'My Book by . . .' and if he can write his name he can write it underneath this. As he does word building he can write the words inside this book and draw or colour any pictures that he needs to go with the words.

Encourage him to take pride in his book, in the way that he write the letters and in his pictures. Praise him for everything that he does and put his book in a very special place. When he has finished his first book, you can staple or sew the pages together.

CHAPTER 4
READY FOR SCHOOL — 4-5 YEARS

Well-balanced and much more mature, your child should be ready for the change from home to school. He should be able to dress and undress himself and socialize well with other children. Basically, he is much more independent and sensible in the way he behaves. Because he understands so much more you can explain more fully and teach him much more.

If he has learned well from the activities in the preceding chapters you will take him through the activities in this chapter with ease, and even go further. You can set about developing his language more fully by encouraging him to choose his own books at the local library, by extending his knowledge of words through word games and puzzles, and by encouraging him to develop an interest in the form of a project and carry it on to the finish.

You will now be able to develop his reasoning powers much further through mathematics and other investigations of the world about him; but you must follow the carefully graded steps in mathematics so that he never attempts an activity without proper grounding. 'Slowly but surely' should be your motto.

Your child is able to express himself more widely in art, music and movement. He will soon be copying shapes well, writing the letters of the alphabet, and will be able to draw most things around him in some recognizable way. He can start very simple stencils now, can colour in crudely, trace a little, make a wide variety of patterns using shapes, and model more real-life objects using Plasticine, clay, Lego and pipe-cleaners.

If he has become a jigsaw addict, the range of twelve piece (and larger) jigsaws (including floor puzzles) is considerable. Finally, you should be able to introduce him to more games: draughts is a must, and also simple card games like Whist.

Of course, these activities will still probably occupy only a small part of his day. He is, for the major part, a physically active, exploring four-year-old.

Development: 4-5 years

- He seems more mature and calm
- He can help around the house and is often very ready for school
- He can climb, hop, slide, swing, and play ball
- He knows his colours and can write most letters well
- He can draw people much better now
- He can dress himself quite well
- He is protective to small animals, sympathetic and sociable

Talking

By this age your child will be doing most of the talking and you will be doing most of the listening! His vocabulary will be increasing by leaps and bounds, as will his understanding of correct grammatical structures.

You can help him increase his vocabulary by talking to him, listening to him, reading to and with him, and making sure he has a plentiful supply of interesting books. Watch television programmes with him and help him to remember some of the technical terms which crop up in documentaries. Play lots of word games with him, let him dictate letters to you, captions for his pictures, written props to accompany games, etc. Make up stories together. If he has heard lots of different stories over the months he will probably be beginning to recognize and repeat some of the classic openings like: 'Once upon a time there lived . . .', etc.

Mathematics

Adding and taking away

In mathematics one of the most important teaching points to remember is that your child needs to consolidate everything he learns. In other words, it is no good his learning about adding up if he does not follow it up for some time afterwards with many activities which remind him how to do it. And even as he learns a new idea (e.g.

taking away) you should still keep reminding him about old ideas (e.g., number symbols, adding up) by including those activities in his mathematics time. Don't assume that he knows for all time how to do something just because he did it well when he was first taught it.

Numbers

Revise and reinforce the games he played in Chapter 3 linking physical objects with number symbols. Play lots of board games like Ludo and Snakes and Ladders where he has to roll a die and move the corresponding number of places. Play games with cards like Sevens where each player has to get rid of his cards by placing the seven of a suit first and then adding either the eight or six of the suit, eventually finishing with an Ace (low) or King (high). Play Rummy where players have to collect three and four of a kind. Here are some suggestions for other useful games:

Dice game

Your child will continue to need lots of practice at linking numbers of objects with the actual number of symbols. One game you can play together which will provide this kind of practice is the dice game.

What you need
A jumbo die, with clearly marked dots; six white cards, each clearly marked with a number from 1 to 6 and the corresponding number of dots beneath it.

What you do
Take it in turns to roll the die. As it comes to rest, look at the number of dots on the face, count them, and then try to find the corresponding card.

Variations
• Use the same cards. Spread them out on the table and ask your child to count out and put the right number of buttons by each card.
• Hold up fingers of one hand. Ask your child to find the

card which corresponds to the number of fingers you are showing.
- Once he is confident about the numbers 1 to 5, introduce 6 to 10, using the same kind of games. If you are playing the dice game, use two dice and just find the two cards which correspond to the two faces showing.

Adding up

Go over the addition cards and simple sums from Chapter 3. Explain again that 'add' and '+' mean the same thing, just like the 'and' in 1 and 5 does. Set out a simple sum with buttons as shown below and talk through it together: 'Three add two makes five'. Then use the number cards and a card with the plus symbol on it to do the sum. Put the cards in the appropriate places and talk through the sum again: 'Three add two makes five'. Then explain that just as the + symbol means the same as 'add', the = symbol means the same as 'makes' or 'equals'. Talk through the sum again! this time ask him to do it. Then put the cards out again, this time including the = card, and go through it again.

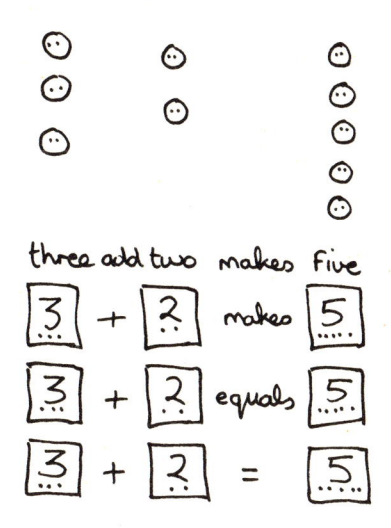

three add two makes five

$\boxed{3} + \boxed{2}$ makes $\boxed{5}$

$\boxed{3} + \boxed{2}$ equals $\boxed{5}$

$\boxed{3} + \boxed{2} = \boxed{5}$

Give him several simple sums to do using first buttons and then cards. It may take some time before he is confident about the different names and symbols. Don't rush him and give him plenty of practice with adding real things.

Then choose a number — for example, 5. Give him five buttons and say: 'Let's find out how many ways we can make five.' Using the buttons, give him a couple of examples: 4+1 and 3+2. Let him put the number cards and the + and = cards underneath each different combination. When he is ready he can then copy down the cards to make a sum, e.g.:

$$4 + 1 = 5 \qquad 3 + 2 = 5$$

When he has exhausted all the possibilities for 5 (it may be a few days, it may be a week) and is very clear about those 'adding up numbers', choose another number between 5 and 10 and repeat the game. Don't spend longer than ten minutes a day on this activity. Make sure he has plenty of concrete experiences to reinforce what he has learnt. Play a game where you sit together and both hold up one hand. Take it in turns to hold up different numbers of fingers: the other person has to say how many are hidden.

Taking away

Play similar games with buttons (or sweets, marbles or spoons) as you did for adding up, and introduce the activity just as slowly. Explain that 'take away' and 'adding up', are both sides of the same coin and talk him through the sums as before

$$5 - 2 = 3$$
$$5 - 3 = 2$$
$$5 - 4 = 1$$
$$5 - 5 = 0 \text{ (nothing or zero)}$$

Some children of this age like to use their fingers. If your child has his own 'way' of adding up or taking away, *don't* stop him whether he uses his fingers, the abacus, other real objects or dots on paper.

Adding and taking away stories

From time to time (at normal storytime), introduce the novelty of number stories. Make up a short story. For example, 'there were four cows in a field. One day a great giant came along and carried off two of them. How many were left?' See if he can make up a little number story of his own. He can even colour or draw a picture of it, or you can do it for him. You could use plastic farm animals and act the story out together!

You can also remind him of classic counting songs by drawing pictures of, for example, ten green bottles.

The adding card game

What you need
Five number cards for each player — use those you made for the dice game.

What you do
Put the cards in a pack. Each person (for example, parent and child) picks two cards. The person with the highest total wins that round and gets *one* point. You have ten rounds, and the person with the most points wins.

You can play this game for taking away. In this case the person with the lowest score each time wins.

Teaching times

What you need
Three toy men, two cards, two toy horses or cows.

What you do
Say: 'Each man has two legs: one, two (pointing). That means that three men have three lots of two legs. That is, 2 add 2 add 2, which is 6.' Repeat with car wheels (two fours) and toy horses (two fours).

Repeat a similar activity with small toys for a few minutes daily and for a couple of weeks. Continue with buttons. Say, as you did with addition, 'Two add two add two equals six.' Ask him to put the cards underneath.

Say: 'Three are three lots of two buttons. You can write this another way – three twos' and write 3 x 2 and then say, pointing to the symbols, 'three times two.'

There are many variations of this multiplying activity using fingers, dots and pictures. Use the variations so that your child is really clear about what multiplication *means*.

The two times table

This activity is not about pressurized learning by rote, because mathematics is, or should be, about *first* understanding, and *second* about practice through an enjoyable activity, a game. Your child will enjoy learning this table *only* if he learns at his own pace.

First: *understanding*

Repeat for 3 x 2, 4 x 2 and 5 x 2, using either pictures, dolls or plastic people.

Second, familiarity
Write the table on a piece of paper in large clear numbers, and stick it up on the bedroom wall or some other prominent place. Go through the table once a day and within a couple of weeks he will know it; but be sure that you also repeat the understanding part, using buttons or plastic people, a couple of times as well in the two weeks.

Sharing

To begin with, play a sharing game together. Share two, four, six sweets between you and your child.

Set up a game that he can play for a few minutes daily, where he shares two, four or six sweets between himself and a teddy bear. Let him spend some days on this. Then let him share between himself and two teddy bears, this time using three, six or nine sweets. Make sure he understands about equal numbers for each. He will need quite some time just playing this game with sweets, biscuits, etc.

Remember: you must always move slowly when a child is first trying to grasp an idea in mathematics.

Other sharing activities
• Let your child learn to share out a few cards for each person for Snap and other card games.
• Show him how to share out cakes and sweets, and other food amongst the members of the family.
• Don't miss out on mentioning half and a quarter when sharing out cake or chocolate. Don't mention other fractions or write down half or quarter; this is for later.
• Make sure that he does some 'sharing' daily because familiarity and practice with these skills is important.

READY FOR SCHOOL – 4-5 YEARS

More about shapes

There are many activities that you can continue with *flat* shapes, especially now he can probably count to ten.

Use sticky paper shapes on blank paper, or draw them. Ask him if he wants to colour them in; ask him to count how many sides they have.

Ask him to watch while you cut four-sided shapes from corner to opposite corner.

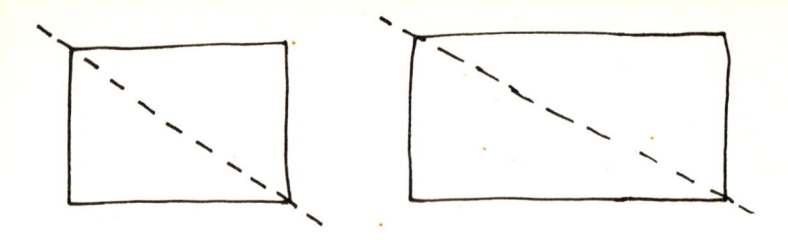

Ask him how many sides the two shapes now have.

Ask your child to see what shapes he can make on a large sheet of paper with triangular shapes. Use the words 'square', 'rectangle', 'triangle' throughout this activity.

Solid shapes

Use wooden bricks to show him a *sphere* a *cube*, a *cuboid*, a *tetrahedron*, a *prism*. When he knows the names, ask him to sort some bricks; 'Can you put spheres here and cubes here?' Ask him to find or name spherical objects in the house, e.g., marble, ball, orange.

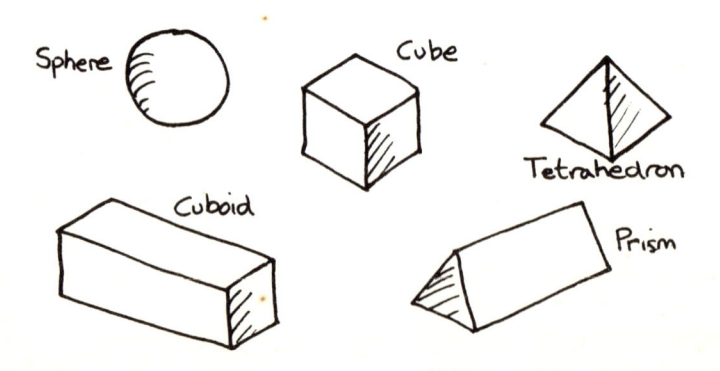

Measurement

Metre stick
Now divide up the metre stick into 100 cms. Colour alternate centimetres and show him what you are doing. Mark off 10, 20, 30, 40, 50, 60, 70, 80, 90, 100 cms.

What to do
Use your metre stick, a ruler with *clear* markings or a clearly marked tape-measure (marked in centimetres only) to measure objects to the *nearest* centimetre (a book, a spoon, the children's heights, their waist measurement, their chest measurement. Write down their personal measurements in a little book – they will be useful anyway). Always show him what you are doing.

Weight
Measure his weight to the *nearest* kilogram. Measure your weight in the same way, and other members of the family. Write down the results in a book and update it every couple of months.

More patterns

You can use buttons to produce sequences for him to continue. For example, ask him: 'What is the next one after this? Can you show me?'

Make the sequence, or pattern, a very simple one and use real objects at this stage.

Dot-to-dot drawings

These are almost creative! Only give him dot-to-dot drawings that are well within his grasp, both in terms of number recognition and drawing skill.

Telling the time

When your child can both count to and recognize numbers from 1 to 12, he may like to begin learning to tell the time.

What you need
A clock with clear numbers on it or a play clock. You can make your own but cardboard play clocks are so cheap it isn't really worth it. The numbers shown should be the cardinal numbers 1, 2, 3, 4, 5, 6, 7, 8, 9, 10, 11, 12.

What to do
First, count round the numbers on the clock-face, pointing to each number in turn. Spend about a week on this. Talk about the different lengths of the hands — one is short and the other is long. Say: 'This is the short hand and this is the long hand.' Then make a game of it by turning the clock-face away from him and saying: 'Now we are going to play a game.' Then turn the clock-face back towards him and say: 'See if you can show me which is the short hand,' and when he has done this say: 'Very good. Now show me which is the long hand.'

Now concentrate on the short hand. Say: 'This small hand shows the hours.' Turn the small hand to each number in turn and say: 'This is one o'clock, this is twelve o'clock', etc. Emphasize that the long hand stays in the same place for the o'clock every time. Repeat this daily until he is very sure of each o'clock in turn.

Now try him with various o'clock times out of sequence. For example, try him with two o'clock and then five o'clock and finally with nine o'clock. If he can't answer immediately, then tell him the answer.

You will need to explain next about morning and afternoon times. This is very important because it gives a sense of the passing of time. What you must do is to relate time to things that he does. For example, at eight o'clock he has breakfast, at one o'clock he has lunch, at four o'clock he has tea and at seven o'clock he goes to bed. So you point to the clock and you say. 'This is seven o'clock. This is when you go to bed. Can you see that the little hand, the short hand, is pointing to the seven and the big hand is straight up? That means that it is seven o'clock in the evening and that is when you go to bed.'

Now explain that morning is before twelve o'clock; then the time starts again for the afternoon. Show the hands of the clock from twelve o'clock midnight through breakfast to twelve o'clock midday, then moving on to one o'clock in the afternoon until twelve o'clock midnight again. You will need to repeat this again and again over the weeks.

Reading

More reading: the local library

Now that you have introduced your child to stories, if you have not already done so, take him along to the library and introduce him to many different books. As you go through enrolling him, explain what you are doing. Make a big fuss of getting him his library card. Tell him how many books he can have out, and for how long. Show him where there are picture books, picture books with words, and story books for young children. Talk to him about the books that he picks up, and try to guide him in making a sensible choice, remembering that, above all, he should have the book that *he* likes and is happy with.

When you get home with his library books, put them in a special place and bring them out at reading time or bedtime, and read the stories with him. If he wants to try to read them to you, give him lots of encouragement as he does so. Remember, don't labour over difficult words – just tell him what they are.

When you go to the library, bring away at least one book about a non-fiction subject, and from time to time bring *this* out to talk about. A favourite subject is animals (sharks, whales, dinosaurs, lions, tigers, elephants), but almost anything will do – space, the milkman, the postman, transport, seaside.

Pre-reading activities

More about phonics: The beginning of words

By now your child should be well used to handling and enjoying all sorts of books. He will understand how books work: that the message or story lies in the words and that reading the words unlocks the meaning. He will probably be very keen to have a go at working out the words for himself. He may well have quite a good sight vocabulary of easy words, and if he has mastered the sounds of individual letters, he may be ready to put letters together in an attempt to work out what a word is.

In the previous chapter he learnt how to use the initial letter of a word as a clue to its sound. Now you can introduce 'blends', i.e., two letters at the beginning of a word which blend together. For example, choose 'c' and 'l' to make 'cl' and ask if he can help you find or make up words: suggest clip, clap, clop, club. Use the single letter cards you made in the previous chapter. Gradually introduce other blends like: 'cr', 'br', 'bl', 'dr', 'fl', 'gr', 'gl', 'pr', 'pl', 'st', 'sp', 'sl', 'tr', 'sw'.

Spend at least a week playing this word game with each double-letter start, and back it up with games like 'I spy' or 'I'm thinking of something beginning with "cl..."'

Word endings

Do the same for word endings: '-ip', '-ag', '-ash', '-op', '-ill', '-og', '-ush', '-ab', '-im', '-in', '-an', '-ink', '-ot'. Please make sure that you approach all this work in a relaxed manner. Spend only a *few minutes per day* on this phonic word building.

Vowel sounds

These letter combinations have a sound all of their own: 'ar', 'or', 'er', 'oo', 'oi', 'ou', 'ear'. Teach them me at a time, very slowly, and gradually make up words in the same way: e.g., car, horn, her, bee, look, food, coin, loud, hear.

Spend some time on each of these in turn, but don't lose sight of your goal: phonic work is not an end in itself, it is just one way among many to enable children to learn to read for themselves. The aim is to read words as part of the message of a book. Phonics is a useful way of working out what the words may be but it is not the only way. Above all it is the sense that matters: there is little point in being able to read each word as an isolated unit and lose the sense in doing so. It is far better for children to understand the sense and make a good guess at a word they can't recognize. And very often phonics will help make the guess more accurate.

So, continue with the reading scheme and all the other books that interest him from the library and the bookshop. Don't overdo the phonics – just make sure that he continues to enjoy reading to you and being read to.

Fitting a word into a sentence

On a large sheet of white paper write clearly: a __ barks. Read it out to him. Say, 'I've missed out something, haven't I? What word goes in there? Is it cat, cow or dog?' Encourage him to put in the right answer, and then read back the sentence to him: 'Yes. Well done. It should be "a dog barks".'

Make up two or three similar sentences. Read them out loud to him (one at a time), tell him the alternative answers and ask him to choose which one he thinks will make sense.

- A __ moos (horse, bird, cow)
- Jack and __ (Fred, John, Jill)
- Bread and __ (cake, mustard, butter)
- The cat is on the __ (rat, hat, mat)

Talk to him about each word so that he chooses the best one. Read the sentence each time with the *wrong* words in the space as well as the right word to show him how silly it can sound.

Make the examples very obvious:

- The plate is on the ___ (floor, bed, table)
- My bed is in the ___ (bathroom, kitchen, bedroom)
- My ___ is Peter (head, name, game)

At this age his sense of humour is well developed, so try to use it.

Simple crosswords

Make sure that the words and clues are very obvious. Draw large-spaced, very clear crosswords.

1. It barks and wags its tail (dog)
2. It moos (cow)

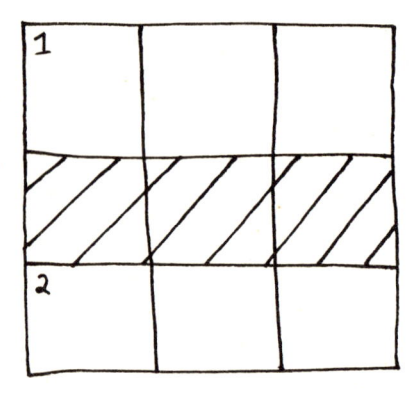

Read the clues to him, talk about possible answers and help him to write in the answers.

Simple spelling

Start with three-letter words that he knows. Choose only one or two a day to help him write down and spell. Say: 'I'm going to say a word, and I want you to see if you can write it down.' (Obviously, this is a 'game' for readers and writers. You should not try a spelling game with non-readers.)

… READY FOR SCHOOL – 4-5 YEARS

Finding out activities

These activities include quite a lot of early mathematics and science work.

Growing seeds

What you need
An eggbox or similar container, cress seeds, sawdust or soil.

What you do
Show your child how you 'plant' the seeds in the sawdust or soil. Leave the container on the kitchen window-sill. Show him how much the cress has grown daily from the first appearance of the shoots. Take out a seedling each day and show him how to measure the growth using centimetres (to the *nearest whole* number.)

Dissolving

Show your child what happens to salt when it is dropped into water. Where does it go? Explain in very simple language about *dissolving*. Do the same with sugar. Experiment with cold and warm water to show how warm water helps substances to *dissolve* quicker.

Freezing water

Show your child how to make ice cubes and 'fruit juice'

cubes in the freezer compartment. Discuss with him what is happening to the water when it is put into the freezer: concentrate on the idea of warm and cold. Arouse his interest by making an ice-lolly.

Heating water

Discuss with him what happens when you heat water.

Watering plants

Show him how to water some indoor plants. Explain *why* we need to water plants indoors. Ask: 'Why don't we always need to water plants outdoors?' It will help his understanding of volume if you use a litre or half-litre jug when watering.

Steam

Get your child to breathe on a mirror. Ask him why it gets cloudy. Explain in terms of *steam* from a kettle.

Air

Discuss with your child how clothes blow on the washing line, smoke trails in the wind, his hair blows in the wind. All these show that there is *air* all about us. Try to get this across to him. Blow up a balloon and talk about what is now inside the balloon (at this age, call it air).

Blow up a balloon and let it go in the back garden.

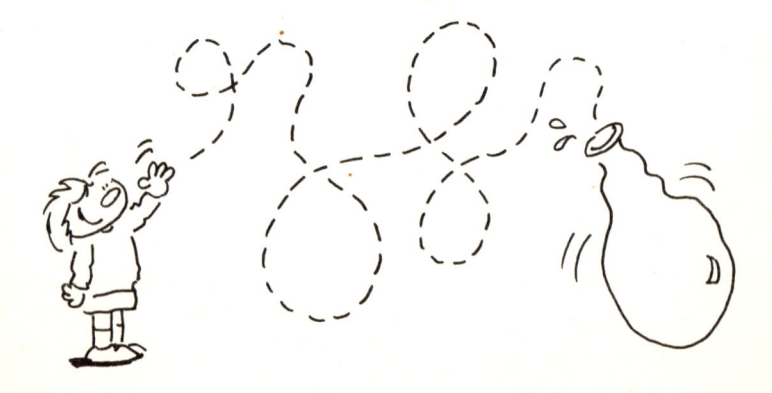

Explain to him as simply as possible what is happening. Say: 'The air in the balloon rushes out and gives *push*.'

Explain about kites. Buy one and help him to fly it.

Making a parachute

What you need
A handkerchief or square piece of cloth, string (four pieces), a metal or plastic figure.

What you do
Tie the string to the four corners of the handkerchief, and the other ends to the toy. Wrap the toy up in the cloth and throw it up in the air (in the garden!) Ask him to guess why it floats down. (This is difficult for even an adult to explain,

Insects

Talk about insects and other small animals that he sees or finds in the house or garden: spiders, beetles, ants, flies, gnats, craneflies. Emphasize how dirty flies are and how they can make food bad to eat.

Magnets

What you need
A magnet from the toy shop, a few iron and steel objects (screws, nuts, paperclips, drawing pins, pins.)

What you do
Leave him to play games with the magnet. This gives him an appreciation of 'invisible forces' in the world.

Cooking

This is a very useful introduction to the idea of quantities. Show him how to make pastry. Stress the amounts of flour, fat, etc. (in grams) that you have to use. After a few weeks you will be able to leave him to make his own jam tarts.

Point out the passing of time by *timing* the cooking. Show him on the clock how many minutes he has to wait.

Trips

Trips to different places of interest — a castle, a market, a farm, a zoo, a pet shop — might encourage him to begin a simple topic. Collect as much information as you can at these places, and at home he can make his own 'book' about it.

Such trips provide endless sources for discussion and plenty of things you may want to follow up together using books from the library.

Displacement of water

Fill a cup with water. Carefully drop a few marbles into the cup. Ask your child to watch what happens and try to explain it. Try to lead him to the idea that the marbles are taking the place of the water that spills over. Mark the level of the bath water before he (or you) gets in. Mark the level once he is in. See if he can explain why it rises.

Seeds

Have a close look at some more vegetables and fruit: orange, banana, tomato, pea, conker, hazelnut. Explain that the seed or nut will become a new plant when it is put into the ground. Plant a conker or bean and see what happens.

Creative games and puzzles

Dice games

If up to now you have helped your child by telling him the scores on a die, now is the time for him to learn how to do it himself. Explain how to score in games like Ludo, Snakes and Ladders: include the throwing of a six and the 'second turn'. To get him used to dice-scoring, play a simple game with him.

What you need
Two dice.

What you do
In turn, each take the two dice and throw them. Get him to add up first his score, and then your score to see who wins on the first throw. Get him to work out, with a little help, who wins after two (or more if he is keen) throws. You should get him to write down the sums on a piece of paper.

$3 + 1 + 2 + 2 = 8$

Other games

Here are other games that you can play with this age group: draughts, Snap, Happy Families, Whist.

Blackboard and easel

What you need
A blackboard (you can make one by painting over a piece of board with blackboard paint), a packet of coloured chalks, a wet rag and a dry rag, thick blank sheets of paper, paints, paint brush, clothes pegs.

What you do
Give him free rein to draw what he likes with chalks. If he prefers to paint, get him to put his 'painting clothes' on and attach the paper to the easel with the clothes pegs. Using an easel allows him to paint outside in the garden as well as inside.

Stencils and tracing

It may help your child to produce more 'realistic' pictures sometimes if he has some stencils; he can then 'colour in' the results. Some children find this very absorbing and satisfying. However, they find tracing much more difficult and you may have to help your child to hold the tracing paper steady as he traces.

Lego and pipe-cleaners

Your child is coming to the age where he is sufficiently

dextrous to be able to fit together Lego pieces, or use pipe-cleaners to make animal shapes. Inititally, though, you must show him how. Keep the models you do for him very simple and easy. Help him with them unless he makes it clear he does not want help.

Clay

To make some 'clay' for him to play with, mix two cups of flour with one cup of salt and knead in water with a little (tablespoon) cooking oil so that you have a dough. Add some food colouring to make red or blue 'clay' (you need very little of this otherwise he will soon have coloured hands!) Leaving the clay open to the warm air hardens it; but if you keep it in a plastic bag in the fridge it will keep fresh for the next play time.

Puzzles

There are many puzzles available on the market for this age and older, but *floor* jigsaw puzzles will always be used. Make sure that the puzzles have very large, thick, cardboard pieces. Try to encourage him to make the puzzles somewhere where they can be left on display for a while.

Jokes

Many children of this age begin to take an interest in simple jokes. Their sense of humour is developing rapidly. They usually love comics and enjoy word games with puns and riddles. Nonsense rhymes and comic verse will also have great appeal.

Pictures and writing

Whenever your child draws or colours a picture, ask him to dictate a caption for you to write underneath it: for example, my house; I go to the shops; I like sweets. Write it for him, explaining about the occasional capitals that you have to print. Then ask him to write over your writing, make sure that he traces over the letters correctly.

After several weeks of tracing over your writing he may want to try to copy what you have written. This is a very demanding task for him to do so make sure that he is under no pressure to tackle more than he enjoys. This activity should make up the majority of his writing effort in any week.

Making a day-to-day story

What you need
Several rectangular sheets of blank paper of the same size.

What you do
Fold the sheets down the middle. Use one at a time to make a page of your child's 'diary'. Spend five or ten minutes every day discussing what he has done or is going to do. Write a sentence for him to trace over (or copy) and

see if he wants to draw or crayon a picture to go with it.

CHAPTER 5
GOING TO SCHOOL —
from 5 years onwards

The age at which your child will be able to begin school varies around the country by as much as one year; some children can start as young as four. This chapter addresses itself to the problem of how you liaise with the school and find out how the infant department caters for the needs of your child. It gives practical advice on how, if necessary, to persuade the teachers that your child is beyond the average level in mathematics and English. It is important that he does not stagnate mentally, so there may be a need for discussion with the staff before he starts school.

You will also need some guidance on how to continue with education at home once your child is at school. How long should you spend with him and when is the best time? How can you best help him to do well at school?

Most parents wish to help their children, in the early years at least, with reading, writing and sums. They need advice on how to solve reading problems and how to help children understand mathematical ideas. By the time he starts school, your child will have had a good grounding in these subjects. This chapter details the steps you need to follow to further your child's mathematical and reasoning ability. It gives suggestions about how you can make him more competent in language. To do this you need spend no more than twenty minutes to half an hour a day with your child; but you must be consistent. Regular, daily learning with you is the key to your child's confidence and his success with his schoolwork.

Talking to the school

Before your child starts school, it is important for you to meet the headteacher to explain how you have helped your child over the past few years. You will also need to talk to the head of the infants' department and the proposed class teacher. Before you set out for any such meetings you should collect together as much information about your child's attainment as possible. Information of most interest to a teacher will be some indication of your child's ability in:

- *Reading* You should show the school what scheme you have used, and whether or not your child can read phonetically. You need to show which particular book he is using in a scheme and what books he reads in general. You should ask for your child to come along to one of these meetings so that the teacher can make his or her own assessment. (Remember, many parents make extravagant claims for their children, which teachers often subsequently find are wild exaggerations.)

Ask if your child can have a reading test if you have not already tested him yourself. (The library will have a section of IQ and reading tests – or the local polytechnic or university will most certainly be able to help.) Some teachers, however, discount some reading tests principally because they do not show whether or not the child understands the *meanings* of words.

- *Writing* It is very important for a class teacher to know what writing activity your child is capable of: can he write odd words (including his name)? Can he copy sentences that you write for him? Whole sentences of his own? Or perhaps even a short set of sentences? You will need to show examples of his work and, better still, get him to write something for his teacher when you all meet. *Remember:* you will need to provide concrete evidence of your child's ability.

• *Mathematics* If your child has faithfully followed the activities outlined in this book, then you will find that he has already participated in many early infant maths activities. You will therefore need to go along to see the class teacher and provide a comprehensive list of what he has done, and how well he understands what he has done. Ask if he can join in with some group activities so that he does not feel 'left out', but also suggest that he needs individual work as well so that his number work can be extended. This does create difficulties for an overworked infant teacher with a large class in which many children have yet to learn to read, so if you have spare time do offer to help read to children, hear them read or help in some other way.

Helping out at school

The school, naturally, will feel more disposed to accommodate your child's special circumstances if you offer help in school-time. Most schools welcome parent-teachers to help children who have reading difficulties, and also any parent who is able to help out with mathematics problems amongst both infants and juniors. The school may also need help with craft, cookery and needlework. Try to become part of the school's co-operative 'team' and before long an indispensable part of school life. Even if you cannot give day-time help, then make yourself an indispensable helper on school trips, the parent-teacher association, jumble sales and sales of work, or you could even become a school governor. The point is that if you take part in school activities you are no longer an 'outsider'. You will understand the pressure of daily school life and you are more likely to be listened to when you need special help for your child. Above all, you must avoid giving the impression that you are in any sense 'criticizing' the efforts of the teachers: make it abundantly clear that you value their expert advice and *need* their help and co-operation for the sake of your child.

Liaison with the school

Individual schools differ in their attitude to parent-teacher relations. If your school welcomes parental involvement then you will be able to follow what your child is doing in class and find out where he needs help at home. If you feel that your work with him at home is racing ahead of his work in class, you should explain to the class teacher what you are doing. Your child will not benefit if the work at school is too easy for him. However, you should bear in mind that the teacher sometimes uses English work for drama, and in this case your child will want to work in a group and not feel the 'odd one out'. Also, some activities involve group work anyway and the emphasis here will be on co-operation. While you are keen to encourage your child's progress as an individual you must allow for his need to work within a group at school, even though sometimes it seems that he is performing activities below his ability. It is important that you should understand the wide variety of activities that your child's school provides that do not directly extend his maths and English, but concentrate more on his social development.

Language and writing

This is the age at which he will be learning to express himself in writing as well as speech.

He may need help with particular types of words, for example, opposite, comparative and superlative adjectives (sweet, sweeter, sweetest), adverbs, etc.

Opposites

One good way for your child to learn words and their meanings is to search for opposites. You can make this a very interesting game. Get him to draw what the words and their opposites mean. Some useful opposites are:

GOING TO SCHOOL – FROM 5 YEARS ONWARDS...

up/down over/under
left/right man/woman
boy/girl father/mother
grandfather/grandmother son/daughter
nephew/niece uncle/aunt
dark/light happy/sad
night/day brother/sister

open/closed tall/short
on/off black/white
fat/thin cold/hot
rough/smooth straight/crooked
hard/soft head/tail
old/young top/bottom
fast/slow in/out

Writing

Your child will now be learning to write at school. He will be writing sentences with his pictures, and perhaps a weekly 'diary'. You can help him by suggesting things to write about in the diary and writing down some of the words that he could use so that he can see the correct spelling (there is no need for him to take them to school).

Sun
Sea-side
Fair
Sand

Ship
Dad
Cross

Capitals and full-stops
Explain that capitals are used for names like Peter, cities like London, and for the start of a sentence. Give a few examples:

> Peter is happy.
> He is happy.

Point out that the full-stop is for the end of a sentence. This reinforces what he will learn at school and you can introduce the complete alphabet of capitals.

A B C D E F G H I J K L M N O P Q R S T U V W X Y Z

Spelling

You should co-operate with the school in giving your child at least five spellings to practise over a week. They should be very simple, no longer than three-letter words. Each 'group' should have similar structures:

- cat, rat, bat, mat, sat, hat
- dog, log, fog, jog
- pit, bit, hit, sit

c <u>at</u>   r <u>at</u>   m <u>at</u>
d <u>og</u>   f <u>og</u>   j <u>og</u>
b <u>it</u>   h <u>it</u>   s <u>it</u>

Mathematics

Difficulties with symbols and words

One of the difficulties with mathematics at any level is that children are confused by symbols and words, and the infant school is no exception.

+, addition, more than
Hopefully, if you have followed the activities in the previous chapter, your child will be very clear about the meaning of 'more than', but you should take many opportunties to give him examples using both this term, '+' and 'add'.

−, subtraction, take away, less than, difference
The first symbol and the next three terms fit in well with the subtraction activities already detailed in this book.

However, there will still be a need to emphasize the words 'subtraction' and 'less than'. A simple way to do this would be to go over the take-away activities and emphasize that these words also apply to them; but you will need to re-emphasize this many times over a period of weeks before he really remembers.

Many books at this level use the word 'difference', which an adult appreciates very well. It attempts to guide the child into a way of subtraction by 'counting on'. This is useful, but can be confusing to a small child because it suggests that 5 − 3 is the same as 3 − 5! In any case, if your local school has books using the term you have to explain it by linking it with other terms like 'taking away' otherwise your child will feel, quite wrongly, that he does not understand subtraction.

Other ways of representing adding and taking away

2 + 4 is another way of representing addition sums and can confuse a child. You may need to explain the meaning of pictures and others like this:

If you are aware of these and other differing approaches, then you can explain to your child that understanding the drawing is different from understanding the maths. He may understand addition well but still be very confused by the book's approach. You must reassure him and give him confidence.

=, equals

Your child needs to appreciate that the = sign is like a weighing balance: what is on the *left* side is balanced by what is on the *right* side:

You can show this with *equal sized* marbles and using a balance. Put three marbles on the left-hand dish and then 'add' two marbles. Show that this can only be 'balanced' by five marbles on the right-hand dish. This is such an important part of mathematics it is worth your child doing sums using marbles and weighing scales for a few minutes a day for several weeks. An equally important idea, which you can show to your child, is that if you take marbles away from the left pan, you must balance the scales by taking away the same number of marbles from the right pan. This concept is used throughout advanced problems in algebra.

Numbers and counting

Your child should by now be clear about numbers between 1 and 20 through writing out simple sums as numbers. However, it is a good idea to write down all the numbers from 1 to 100 clearly on a large sheet of paper. From time to time you can refer to the sheet (perhaps pinned up on his bedroom wall) and count some of the numbers with him.

Use of the blank space, the placeholder, in books
Sums in books can be written

$$3 + 2 =$$

This is fairly straightforward, but your child may experience more difficulty with

$$2 + \square = 3$$

To emphasize what this means say: 'This means two add *something*, we don't know what, is equal to three. Put the right number in the placeholder, the box.'

In general

If there are any difficulties with words or symbols in school books, you should discuss them with the class teacher, ideally *before* your child meets them in a lesson. If you do this, then he will not be faced with failure, and with maths a sense of failure leads to a dislike of the subject and the feeling that 'I just can't do "maths".'

Measurement

Life is very confusing for a small child. When he goes to the shops he buys a 'quarter' of sweets, two pounds of potatoes, a pint of milk and it is half a mile to walk back home. At school, he learns only metric measures – centimetres, grams and litres. The only solution to the problem is to explain that both systems are used. You can point out that on the sides of packets of food it gives weight in kilograms and pounds, and cartons of liquids give both litres and pints.

However, since the school will emphasize metric measures in mathematics, you can concentrate on ironing out any problems he has. And some of the units do pose problems: millilitres and grams are too small for an infant to measure, so weight measures should be 100 grams, 200 grams, 500 grams, one kilogram; and volume 100ml, 200ml, 500ml, and 1 litre. Your child will need as much practical experience as possible. You should continue emphasizing volumes of water and milk used in cooking and on cartons of yogurt and orange juice. Show him the measures that you use with a jug. Sugar, margarine, flour and other foods have weights written on them, and you should let your child use the weighing scales to check the weights. It should help if you write a notice and pin it up somewhere in the kitchen:

Measuring distance is easier: for a few minutes each day ask your child to do some measuring using a metre stick, a tape measure or a clearly marked ruler:

Make the measurements as useful as possible – measure height, waist or chest measurements and put them into a 'measurement book' that your child can put away in his own drawer.

Guessing games about measurements also stimulate interest. For example, you might ask: 'What height do you think the door is? What height of man could just walk through it without bumping his head?' and 'How long is a bus?'

Telling the time

There is so much to learn here that your child's teacher will be thrilled if he can 'tell the time', even if he can just do the hours and half-hours.

Now your child has started school he will be much more aware of time: the time he has to get up, the time school starts, playtime, dinnertime, hometime, bedtime all take on a new significance.

He may well now want to learn to tell the time, if he has not already done so. For activities to teach the hours see pp. 116–17. Once he has really mastered these (which may take days, weeks or months), you can teach him the half hour.

Show him the clock at half-past two, for example, say to him: 'The little hand points to the two and the long hand points straight down: this says half-past two. See if you can say it after me.' Repeat this for half-past three, half-past four and half-past all the hours. When you have done all the half-pasts try him with a few of them and see if he can give the correct answer. If he can't, tell him the answer, 'Well done, that's a good try', and leave the activity until the next day. If he is very keen and wants to go on trying then carry on.

When he is very clear about the half-past times you can go on to the quarter-past first and the quarter-to times, but don't rush it. Make sure that he is very clear about one skill before you move onto the next. Many children will not be ready for this activity until they are six or seven years old. If your child shows any signs of difficulty, leave it for another six months or a year.

Sharing

Your child will be very confused by the symbols used unless you can give him clear guidance. Even if he understands very well what sharing *is*, he will need much practice with sums written in different forms: 8 divided by 2, 8 divided by two, shared amongst two. The inevitable question is: 'which are the sweets and which are the men

to share them with?' To overcome this difficulty you will need to set him a few sums a day over a period of weeks until he has cleared up the confusion in his mind:
- 10 sweets shared amongst 2 people is ?
- 10 divided by 2 is ?
- How many twos in 10 ?
- Divide a set of 10 into sub sets of 2:

You will need to explain the meaning of the word *set* (a group of several of the same things.)
- Match equal numbers of sweets for each person.

Times tables

The school would be very happy for you to extend your child's times tables. If he knows the 2x table, then do the 10x table next. Write it out clearly on a large, blank sheet of paper, explaining to him the meaning of the sums, for example: '10 x 2 = 20. This means that two lots of 10 make 20, 10 add 10 makes twenty, and also 10 lots of 2 make twenty – 2 + 2 + 2 + 2 + 2 + 2 + 2 + 2 + 2 + 2 makes 20!' Let him check the sums with his buttons. Pin the tables sheet up where he can see it easily (again, in the bedroom is best) and periodically go through it until he knows it well. Approach table learning as a game,

and spend only a few minutes on it in a day.
   You can later go through other tables in a similar way. Do the 5x table next, and then 3x, 4x, 6x, 7x, 8x and 9x.

1x3   2x3   3x3   3x3   4x3

Take your time over teaching him his tables. It may take a year, although some very young children with excellent memories can learn much quicker. John learnt all his tables (1x to 10x) perfectly in a few weeks when he was three-and-a-half years old. He enjoyed learning them immensely, but as a rule it is best to spread out the learning time.

Right angles

What you need
A sheet of rectangular paper.

What you do
Fold the paper once so that there are two halves, and then fold across this fold to produce four quarters.
   Explain that a right angle is like turning round a corner, and trace your finger around the 'corner' of the right angle. Ask him to find other right angles in the house: the corner of a book, of the door, the table, the window.
   Teaching the points of the compass is an excellent way of explaining about right angles.

What you need
A compass, a large sheet of paper, crayons or chalk.

What you do
Show him how to find north with the compass. Explain where the points of the compass are – north, south, east and west – and draw the points either on the path outside or on the paper. Standing him in the centre and face him north: if he turns to east or to west he turns one right angle:

Extend his variety of experiences of right angles by using squares, rectangles and right-angled triangles.

Symmetry

Small children like to find symmetry in shapes. Explain that if something is symmetrical, when it is cut in half, the two halves will be the same.

What you need
Rectangular or square sheets of paper.

What you do
Ask him to fold the sheet of paper so that he forms two equal halves.

Write out some of the capital letters of the alphabet, and ask him to find the lines of symmetry. If he finds it difficult, don't persist, but some small children find this activity extremely enjoyable.

Point out to him that lines of symmetry can be horizontal as well as vertical: 'Let's try C now. Can we draw the line from the top to the bottom? No – it doesn't work does it. What about if we draw it across the middle?'

Also, give him plenty of practical experience with cutting slices of bread, oranges, apples, hard-boiled eggs in half. Show him how to make 'butterfly' pictures by painting on one side of a piece of paper, then folding and pressing to produce the design on the other half.

Area

What you need
Centimetre square graph paper, some flat cardboard or plastic shapes (squares, rectangles) which will fit the graph paper.

What you do
Ask your child to choose one of the shapes and put it on the graph paper. Show him how to draw round it and then lift it up and shade in all the squares it covered. Ask him to count the number of shaded squares. Tell him: 'You counted twelve squares. This means that the area is twelve centimetres squared.'

Let him go on to do the same with the other shapes.

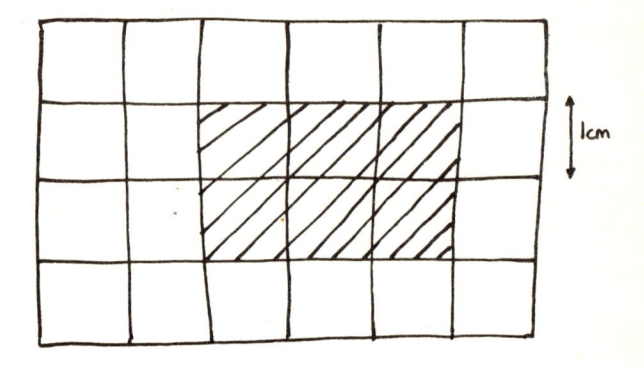

Money
When you go to the shops give your child 10p and send him to buy some penny sweets. Help him to sort out his change. Be patient with him at the check-out (and hope that the cashier is too!) If he still has considerable difficulty with shopping then play 'shops' at home with him for a couple of times a week until he is clear about what he is doing. Shopping is one of a child's favourite games, so you have his interest from the beginning!

Money 2
When your child can count to at least twenty lay out on the table 1p, 2p, 5p and 10p coins as shown in the picture.

Say to him, pointing to the 2p coin: 'This is the same as two of these' — pointing to the 1p coins. Then point to the 5p coin and say: 'This is the same as five of these' — again, pointing to the 1p coins. Then point to the 10p coin and say: 'This is the same as ten of these' — 1p coins. Then say: 'Now we are going to play a game.' Put all the 1p coins in one pile then take a 2p coin and say: 'How many of those can I get for this?' If he can't answer straightaway then show him. Then do the same with the 5p and 10p. Try the same activity for several days. Don't be too impatient with him, because it is difficult for him to recognize that one 2p coin is the same as two 1p coins. If it is very obvious that he has no idea of exchange then leave this activity for a while.

Using a calculator
When your child is really confident and clear about the + sign, show him how to do simple addition sums on the calculator. To begin with, use it only to check sums he has completed successfully. Then give him sums to do on paper which he can then check on the calculator. Eventually he will be able to work straight on the calculator.

When he is equally confident about subtraction and the − sign, show him how to do these kind of sums on the calculator.

Reading

Most schools are happy to allow children to take their reading books home, especially if they know that parents will regularly hear their child read. At this stage make a point of concentrating on any words that are giving him particular trouble.

Whatever his school reading schedule, continue to encourage his general reading at home, both of books bought from bookshops and borrowed from libraries. Maintain an interest in what he is reading, ask questions about the stories and check with him about words or phrases that he is not clear about. And, of course, keep reading to him yourself.

'Sentence blanks'

'Sentence blanks' are an enjoyable way of teaching your child an important early reading skill — intelligent guessing. If he comes across a word he cannot read, very often the context of the word will enable him to make a good guess as to what it may be. If he can recognize the inititial letter, this will provide another clue. Encourage him to guess words when you read together.

There is a wealth of good workbooks for children of this age. Choose those that have graded examples where sentences have 'blanks' to be filled in. For example:
An eagle is a __ (fish, bird, aeroplane)
A cow is an __ (apple, car, animal)

This type of activity, carefully graded to match your child's ability, will greatly extend his *general knowledge* as well as his vocabulary. If he enjoys this activity then set your own examples:
The __ is an animal that gives us milk (horse, cow, chicken)
I laugh because I am __ (sad, happy, cross)

Sometimes, you may need to read out the sentences and the words in brackets, and ask him to choose the correct word.

Simple word games

'Scrabble'

What you need
Cut-out letters from card or stiff paper (toy shops sell sets of letters).

What you do
Put the letters in a cardboard box. Ask your child to take out four letters without looking and try to make a word with two, or even three of the letters (help him if he has difficulty.) The next player takes four letters and again tries to make a word. Each player takes a letter in turn until someone can make a word. The first person to make a word wins the round.

Jumbled words
Simple anagrams can also be a help in learning spelling. For example:

>WCO is COW
>DBE is BED

These types of activities should always be found in any good workbook.

Crosswords

¹C	O	W²
A	▨	E
³T	▨	T

A note on handwriting

At this age do not emphasize neatness too much. Your child needs practice at forming letters, and at home he should be encouraged to write letters and words when he is keen to do so. Let him repeat letters over and over again, especially those that are formed with the same type of movement. Avoid the restrictions of lined paper – let him spread his practice over a large sheet of blank paper.

If he wants to write more, then perhaps he can write a letter to Grandma, to Father Christmas, to a TV competition (with your help). Perhaps he will want to draw pictures about Christmas or his birthday and write some captions. Very often small children want to write in the scrapbooks that they build up. Then there are lists: of toys for Christmas and birthdays, of things to buy at the shops, of New Year's resolutions (again, with your help). Just make sure that he is writing the letters correctly, and leave him to it.

Topics and finding-out activities

For topic work and finding-out activities you will need your own reference library of books on every conceivable subject. You can, of course, always use the local library, but there is no substitute for books which are to hand in the home. In this way, your child can continue a topic or finding-out activity set at school as soon as he gets home. Living in a village as we do, and far from a library, that stock of reference books was invaluable. It was built up from hours upon hours of browsing at jumble sales and fêtes, so that there was at least one book on every subject that I could think of.

Small children are always looking for a book on something that has caught their interest, sparked off by a television programme, a lesson at school, or just a conversation with a friend. There are so many topics: here are just a few which my children enjoyed — dinosaurs, whales, sharks, snakes, travel, crocodiles, castles, cars, aeroplanes, bridges, countries, football, cricket, athletics, any other sport, dancing, ships, cartoon characters, space and rockets, fish, birds, flowers, trees, collecting things, clothes of the past, trains, farms, zoos, the jungle, TV characters, film characters, clouds, hurricanes, the biggest and smallest, the Romans, Normans, Stone Age, etc.

Home topics

Perhaps you could suggest a topic for him to start in the holidays. This could involve cutting out pictures, drawing, painting, writing and even modelling in clay or with paper. A topic on aeroplanes can lead to experiments to find the best aeroplane to do aerobatics, for example.

School topics

When the school sets him a topic you can encourage his interest by finding books for him, taking him to museums to see the real thing (e.g., whales and dinosaurs at the Natural History Museum), making a note of any television or radio programmes which might be of interest.

Other ways in which you can help are by finding out whether he needs:
- any objects collected from home;
- help with vocabulary or spelling;
- further explanation about anything;
- help with any problems so that he feels confident about what he is trying to do.

Out-of-school activities

Chess

You may think that at five or six years of age your child is too young for chess. However, many young children find draughts and chess absorbing and if they do show great keenness, take them along to the local chess club (especially if it has a junior section.) Perhaps other members of the family have some expertise and can pass it on, but in any case there are both excellent junior teaching books and computer chess games to further his interest. (Computer chess, however, often requires learning a complicated symbolic system.)

Board games

- *Darts* will further his ability to add scores mentally.
- *Monopoly* — the 'banker' must be very competent with large numbers.
- *Cluedo* — a test of reasoning and deductive powers, and a game which also requires a good memory.
- *Junior Scrabble* — your child will need help, but his spelling will improve and he will learn to look up words in a dictionary.

Card games

These give practice in matching, sorting into groups and also counting. A player learns to put cards into an order and to memorize what cards have been laid and; he learns to share equally amongst players. Start with simple games like Snap, Happy Families, Whist and move on to Sevens, Patience, etc.

Games of chance

These develop the ability to assess probabilities – an aspect of mathematics which comes into many card and dice games. You should point out the odds in the games that you play, starting with simple odds (for example, the odds of a diamond being dealt first is 1 in 4).

Learning a language

If your child's primary school teaches a language then you can give support at home. Ask your child to talk about what he did at school, and see if he can remember any words that he learnt. As often as not he will not want to go over any schoolwork, so just leave it for now.

If the school does not teach any languages at this age, try him with French or Spanish at home. Say to him: 'Perhaps we will go on holiday to Spain. Shall we learn some words that they say?' Your local library will be able to provide you with cassettes, records and books. Try him with a few words a day – counting, for example, at the beginning. If you want to learn as well, you can learn together. Start with everyday conversation:

'Bonjour, John, comment va-tu?'
'Je vais très bien, merci.'

This conversational way of learning is more fun. Don't introduce grammar for some time, but do teach the days of the week, the months of the year, the weather, so that you can at least mention what day it is.

Finally, when choosing a language remember that some are easier to learn than others: choose Spanish or French in preference to Russian or Chinese!

Learning to play an instrument

If your child has a good ear for music, has always taken an interest in songs, and perhaps could sing in tune as a toddler, then he may want to learn to play tunes on the piano or recorder. You may be able to teach him yourself. Early teaching books give extremely clear guidelines, and all you have to do is to follow simple instructions, and your five- or six-year-old will soon be playing recognizable tunes. Perhaps it will help if you learn along with him.

Be careful in your choice of instrument, though. It may be easy to start on the piano, but at this age the violin, even the early stages, takes some mastering!

IN THE FINAL ANALYSIS

If your child has followed the activities in the previous chapters, and has played freely for the major part of his pre-school and early school life, then he will be, to all outward appearances, a normal healthy child, sociable and with a wide variety of interests. He will have a keen, enquiring mind; he will reason and read and write well and have a firm grasp of mathematical ideas. Good co-operation between the school and yourself will enable him to further satisfy his intellectual needs. He will be happy physically and mentally and, above all, will be confident in the face of challenges in and out of school.

Index

acting, 39-40, 69, 100
activities, out of school, 151-4
addition, 83-6, 105-6, 107
   card game, 109-110
   cards, 85
   difficulty with symbol and words, 136
   other ways of representing, 137-8
   stories, 109
   using bricks, 83-4
   using buttons, 84-5
   using fingers, 84
air, 122-3
angles, 143-4
area, 146

benefits of teaching your child at home, 10-13
blackboard and easel, 127
blank space, use of in mathematics, 139
blowing through a straw, 66
board games, 152
book, your child's first (handwritten), 102
books, 28
   choosing, 28-9
   pictures in, 29
bricks, use of in mathematics, 78
bridge building, 19, 26, 52-3
bubbles, playing with, 64
building
   a bridge, 19, 26, 52-3
   a tower, 14, 19, 25, 42

calculator, using a, 147
capitals, 135-6
card games, 54-5, 104, 152
chess, 151-2
clapping songs, 71
clay, modelling with, 128
collage, make a, 98
colour cards, 44
colouring, 97
colours, 44
compass, points of the, 144
'concrete' experience, 18, 26
cooking, 124
counting
   at home, 41
   on fingers, 41
   practice, 81-2
   rhymes, 87-8
   use of games for, 73
   use of rhymes for, 72-3
   with an abacus, 72
   with buttons, 72
creative play, 38-41, 68-71, 97-102
crockery, 55
crosswords, simply, 120, 149

dancing, 40, 69
development
   0-2 years, 20
   2-3 years, 51
   3-4 years, 75-6
   4-5 years, 104
   key factors, 18
   of intelligence, 10
dice games, 106-7, 126-7

displacement of water, 125
dissection, 67
dissolving, 121
division, 112-13, 141-2
dominoes, 73
dot-to-dot drawings, 116
drawings, 38-9, 68-9, 97
    dot-to-dot, 116
dressing-up, 39-40, 100
    clothes, 40

Einstein, Albert, 11
environment, discovering the, 96
equals (=), 138

feeling things, 67
finding out activities, 95-7, 121-6, 150-54
freezing water, 121-2
full stops, 135-6

games of chance, 152
group activities, importance of, 12
growing seeds, 121, 126

hands, 66
handwriting, 149-50
heating water, 122

idea of comparative size, 14-15, 23-6
insects, 124
instrument, learning to play, 99, 153-4

jigsaw puzzles, 46-8, 74
jokes, 128
jumbled words, 149

labelling cards, 43
language
    and writing, 134-6
    development of, 10
    learning a foreign, 153
learning to play an instrument, 99, 153-4
Lego and pipe-cleaners, 127
library, local, 117-18

making faces, 69
magnets, 124
marbles, 37
matching
    cards, 79
    colours, 77-8
    length, 78
    shapes, 79
mathematics, 77-90, 105-117, 133
    difficulties with symbols and words, 136-9
    use of the blank space (placeholder), 139
measurement, 74, 88-90, 115, 139-41
    length, 88-9
    use of imperial or metric, 139
    volume, 89-90
    weight, 90, 115
metre stick, 74, 115, 140
    making a, 89
missing toy game, 46
missing word game, 119-20
money, 83, 146-7
multiplication, 110-12
music, 41, 70, 98-9
    game, 99

name tags, 43
naming words, 21
number cards, 73, 82
number games
    with buttons, 82
    with fingers, 82
    with sweets, 82
numbers, 82, 106-7, 138
nursery rhymes, 32-3, 91
    games using, 91
nursery school, choice of a, 76

opposites, 134-5
ordering
    by size, 24-5
    with shapes, 81
    with straws, 80-81
    with toys, 81

painting, 38-9, 68, 97
pairing objects, 55-6, 80
parachute, making a, 123-4

INDEX

patterns, 115
pets, 96-7
phonics, 92
    beginnings of words, 118
    endings of words, 118
    games for teaching, 92-4
    vowel sounds, 118-19
pictures, 129
pipe-cleaners, 128
placeholder (the blank space), use of in mathematics, 139
plants, watering, 122
Plasticine, 36-7, 76, 98, 104
play activities, 10, 12, 22-6
Play-Doh, 36-7
playing with
    bricks, 22-6
    posting box, 22-6
poetry, 58-9
pots, pans and wooden spoons, 37
pre-reading activities, 33, 59-61, 92, 118-19
problem-solving, 45-8, 74
puzzles, 74, 128

reading
    assessment before starting school, 132
    cards, 34, 60-61
    scheme choices, 61-3
    to your child, 28-30, 58, 90-91, 147-50
    where and when, 29-30
    with your child, 94-5
records, 33-40
reflections, 67
rhymes, 30-32, 76
    use in learning to count, 72-3, 87-8
rhyming words, 92
right angles, 143-4
role playing, 69

sand, playing with, 36
school
    helping out at, 133
    liaison with the, 134
    talking to the, 132-3
scissors, using, 68, 97

seeds, growing, 121, 126
sense of humour, 45-6
'sentence blanks', 148
shapes, 88, 113-14
    solid, 114
sharing, 112-13, 141
shopping, 83
size
    concept of, 23-6
    ordering by, 24-5
Snakes and Ladders, 73
songs, use of, 26, 28, 71, 99-100
    clapping, 71
sorting, 26-7
    by colour, 27, 57
    by pattern, 27
    by shape, 26-7, 57
    clothes, 53-4
    letters from numbers, 79-80
    toys, 56
spelling, 136
    simple, 120
steam, 122
stencils and tracing, 127
sticky-shape pictures, 39, 57
story, making a day-to-day, 129-30
straws, use of in mathematics, 78, 80-81
structured play, 18
subtraction, 105-6, 108-9
    difficulty with symbol and words, 136-7
    other ways of representing, 137-8
    stories, 109
    using buttons, 86-7
    using fingers, 87
Sunday school, 76
symmetry, 145

taking away, 86-7, 105-6, 108-9
    difficulty with symbol and words, 136-7
    other ways of representing, 137-8
    stories, 109
talking
    0-2 years, 20-21
    2-3 years, 51

3-4 years, 76-7
　　　4-5 years, 105
tapes, 33, 40
television programmes, 33, 96
telling the time, 116-17, 141
times tables, teaching, 110-11,
　　142-3
topics
　　home, 151
　　school, 151
tower building, 14, 19, 25, 42, 53
toy cars, 37
trips (outings), 124
two times table, 111-12

using your ears, 52, 67
using your eyes, 52, 67

water
　　heating, 122
　　displacement of, 125
　　playing with, 35, 63
weighing balance, how to make
　　a, 65
weights, 64-5
word games, 148-9
words, jumbled, 149
writing, 100-102, 135
　　assessment before starting
　　　school, 132-3
　　language and, 134-6
　　name, 101-102
　　patterns for, 100-101
　　pictures and, 129
　　tracing letters, 101

zero, use of, 87